HOW TO

YOUR SERIOUS STEP-BY-STEP BLUEPRINT

WRITE

FOR CREATING INCREDIBLY, IRRESISTIBLY,

FUNNY

SUCCESSFULLY HILARIOUS WRITING

For the laffers

Also by Scott Dikkers

BOOK **1**

HOW TO

YOUR SERIOUS STEP-BY-STEP BLUEPRINT

WRITE

FOR CREATING INCREDIBLY, IRRESISTIBLY,

FUNNY

SUCCESSFULLY HILARIOUS WRITING

SCOTT DIKKERS

TABLE OF CONTENTS

A friend once asked me what comedy was. That floored me. What is comedy? I don't know. Does anybody? Can you define it? All I know is that I learned how to get laughs, and that's all I know about it. You have to learn what people will laugh at, then proceed accordingly.

— STAN LAUREL

1

INTRODUCTION

When you get pulled into a good piece of humor writing, something magical happens. The string of words in front of you ignites a spark that sends outlandish images and funny ideas racing into your brain like a lit fuse, culminating in an explosion of laughter.

Most of us don't have a clue what's making us laugh, exactly. We can't articulate it. "I don't know—I just thought it was funny," we say.

Maybe it's the headline, or the tone, or a great joke in the first few lines. Maybe it's the crazy characters or escalating absurdity, or the way the writer strings it all together to make you see the world or yourself with a skewed perspective that you've never experienced before.

Whatever it is, when you put down that story, lean back in your chair and wipe away the tears of laughter, one thing is certain. You've just enjoyed a rare treat—the polished work of a master humor writer.

It's a rare treat. There aren't many great pure-prose humor writers in the world. You could probably count the ones who've made you laugh out loud on one hand. There haven't even been that many throughout history. It's a one-in-a-million writer who can elicit sustained, hardy laughs from total strangers with nothing more than words on a page.

Why is that? Why are there so few writers who can do this? I'll tell you why. Because writing humor that's funny—really, gut-bustingly funny— is one of the most difficult and challenging literary crafts.

Other genres of writing, by comparison, are easy.

A horror story, for example, is extremely easy. You could probably write a pretty good one over a weekend, like Stephen King frequently does. Vampires, ghosts, blood, screaming, and a slew of other pre-vetted, inherently spooky clichés are sitting on the horror tool shelf waiting to be dusted off whenever a writer needs to drum up a scare.

A story that's a good cry is easy, too. Write about a pet dog or a beloved horse that dies, or a couple who splits up, or a kid yanked from his mother's arms. Separate some characters who are meant to be together, or kill them off before their time, when others are depending on them. Writing a story that makes readers cry is like pushing a button.

But what if you want to make readers laugh?

Maybe you can re-tell that great joke you heard the other day. No, wait, you can't do that—that would be stealing.

Maybe you can tell a story from your life that you found hilarious. But, on second thought, most people probably won't find that funny. It's one of those "you had to be there" situations. Most funny stories from life are like that.

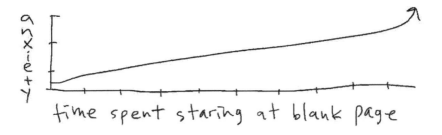

In fact, all the go-to funny ideas you can think of have been done to death: banana-peel slipping, mothers-in-law, three somethings walk into a bar . . . How do you think of something new that's funny? How do you create laughs out of thin air—and somehow transfer them perfectly onto a blank page?

We can scarcely explain why we laugh at funny writing. How can we possibly be expected to create it?

Where do we even start?

We start here.

To paraphrase E. B. White, comedy is like a frog—once you start dissecting it, it's not funny. And dissecting comedy and the comedy-writing process is exactly what we're going to do in this book.

So, get out your scalpel. In order to figure out how to write funny, we have to take it apart, analyze it, and learn how to put it back together.

It's not going to be an easy task. It may not even be funny. But rest assured, the end result will be you getting a lot better at writing things that make people laugh.

WHAT IS FUNNY?

To begin to understand how to make people laugh, we first have to ask, what is laughter, how does it work, and what makes people do it?

Peter McGraw is a professor of marketing and psychology at the University of Colorado Boulder. He believes he's discovered the unified field theory of humor. He can explain what's funny with a simple Venn diagram showing how a "benign violation" is always funny.

Comedy teacher and Hollywood script doctor Steve Kaplan believes he's reduced the definition of all comedy down to one sentence that screenwriters and performers can use to generate laughs in movies or TV shows: an ill-equipped relatable character who faces impossible odds yet doesn't give up.

Psychologists have a lot of theories as to why people laugh: it's a gesture of submission in a complex interpersonal dynamic; it's the result of a positive state; it's the brain processing an error in stimuli; it's any number of other nuanced, involuntary, intellectual or social responses.

The ideas of these modern experts, as well as those of the philosophers and thinkers who've braved this topic throughout the eons, provide some insight into what makes people laugh. But such intellectual humor analysis usually attempts to define only things that are funny in two areas: real life and performance.

The question for us is, how do you *write* something funny? In writing, there's no funny performer or engaging personality to "sell" the humor. This salesperson is a critical tool almost all humor takes advantage of. People like people. They like watching funny people perform for them. They like when Uncle Bob tells one of his great yarns, or when their favorite celebrity comedian comes out with a new movie or new bit.

When audiences *read* something funny, there's nobody there. There's no funny face you love, no familiar voice. There's just a page or a screen sitting there, lifeless. A bunch of symbols.

Furthermore, there's no sound. There's no image. There's not even time or space in which timing can be controlled in order for an act of comedy to take place. There's just a big block of intimidating gray copy.

So, how do you write humor when it seems you have no tools to do so?

THE HUMOR WRITING TOOLS

We've all heard that humor is a matter of personal taste. What makes one person laugh is different from what makes another person laugh, and there's no predicting what people will find funny.

Let's say for a moment that's true. There are no objective standards in comedy. That means no one has a better chance of making people laugh than anyone else. Professional comedy writers are on a level playing field with anybody off the street—everybody's a comedian, tossing off jokes and hoping some of them stick, not having any idea which jokes will get laughs and which won't.

Obviously, that's not how it works. Professional comedy writers have a very good idea what's going to work. It's their job, and they need to be able to do it consistently. And they do it by using special tools, just like plumbers or drywall contractors use special tools to do their jobs.

While the tools of the humor writer aren't in a physical toolbox, they're no less real and essential for the job. Each one has its own specific function. To write humor in a reliable and repeatable way, the professional comedy writer reaches for these tools like you would a trusty hammer or screwdriver.

That said, a lot of comedy writers don't have a clear idea what these tools of humor look like, and would be hard-pressed to explain how to use them. They've probably never thought about it. They don't have to—they only need to be able to use the tools themselves. Most of them developed the tools and the skills to use them over a lifetime of trial and error, practice, dogged persistence, or all the above. Using them has become second nature to them.

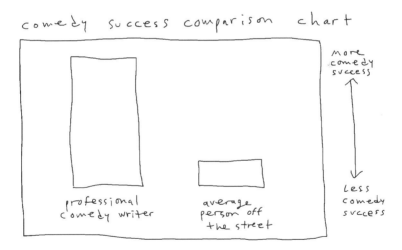

Every successful comedy writer uses these tools. Some writers favor some tools over others, but all the tools in the toolbox are the same.

This book is going to describe those tools in detail and explain how to use them. It's going to condense everything the typical comedy writer or funny person learns about comedy through trial and error throughout his or her lifetime until it becomes instinct, and it's going to distill that knowledge into a guided process that you can learn.

All the tools of the professional comedy writer, as well as specific instructions for how to use them, are now yours.

These tools will not work all the time, but they will work most of the time. And that's the best you can get in humor writing. Yes, this is an objective craft, but it's not math or science. It's entertainment. You will bomb sometimes.

There's a difference between a professional comedy writer and a random person off the street: a professional comedy writer's material works more often than the non-professional's. There are fewer mistakes. A writer whose humor succeeds most of the time is considered an outstanding success by any standard. In this way, comedy is more like baseball than brain surgery. You might lose more than you win, but you can still maintain a solid batting average. And the good news is, in comedy writing nobody dies when you make a mistake.

But hold on. Being funny is something you're born with, isn't it? You can't teach this stuff. You're either funny or you're not. Right?

I've been hearing this conventional wisdom for years. And through those years, I've seen not-very-funny writers—myself included—work hard, apply themselves, and then transform into the most celebrated comedy writers in the world.

When I first got interested in writing humor, I was terminally unfunny, crushingly shy, and always the least charismatic person in the room. Performing was out of the question. Writing, however, seemed within my reach. The problem was, my writing was bad. I had trouble generating my own ideas. I couldn't spell. Much of my early work simply aped the writing I'd seen in *Mad* magazine.

I read whatever I could get my hands on. I craved information about how to write funnier jokes, snappier dialogue, and laugh-out-loud stories. This was before the Internet, and I didn't know anyone who knew how to write comedy. At my local library, there were no how-to books on writing jokes or funny stories. They had only one book in their "Arts & Recreation" section: *How to Be a Ventriloquist.*

What I wanted was a book that explained the tools that professional funny people use. I wanted to use established techniques to make my writing funnier. I eventually found prolific author and original *Tonight Show* host Steve Allen's *How to Be Funny*, but it's not exactly a how-to guide. It's just disjointed interviews with him transcribed by a secretary—more a collection of his humor philosophy than any kind of guidebook.

The craft of comedy has been treated, for a long time, almost like the craft of magic. "A magician never reveals his tricks," is how the magician's creed goes. But magicians have nothing on comedy writers. Plenty of magicians explain their tricks in books and magic kits you can buy. When I was a kid, I could buy how-to magic books and magic kits at any novelty store. Not so with comedy. Those tricks are never revealed. They've been in a vault. Traditionally, the only way to learn them was decades of practice. You just had to figure it out for yourself.

Until recently.

Fifty years ago, the Second City in Chicago started teaching people how to perform comedy, and their impressive list of graduates is proof enough that comedy can in fact be taught. They began teaching writing a few decades later, and have since prepared writers for a lot of the top TV comedy shows.

Comedian Louie Anderson started a stand-up boot camp where he and others taught the art of stand-up comedy.

Colleges are starting to take comedy seriously as well. Academically focused comedy-writing classes are popping up at prestigious universities everywhere.

But unless you go to one of those schools, there's no divining the skills of humor writing. I'm writing this book in an attempt to create the kind of simple, one-stop, tell-all, how-to book that I was looking for when I was starting out.

Comedy writing is a craft. It can be learned, it doesn't have to take decades, and it doesn't have to be frustrating or isolating.

Finding humor happens in a split second. Your mind makes a connection, it squares with your internal notion of what's funny, then you write it down or say it. Everyone's sense of humor is unique, but everyone who's funny—or has ever said or done anything funny—has followed these same fundamental steps to create that funny moment.

In this book, those quantum, incremental steps that take place in that split second are laid out in the form of a clear blueprint that anyone can learn, practice, then master.

> FUNNY-WRITING TIP #1: CONCEPT IS KING
>
> *When you write humor, the core concept you're writing about has to be funny. The core concept is, in fact, the most important part of your writing. So, you need to get it right. The greatest, funniest writing in the world will not save a bad concept. But a great concept written even barely adequately will often be met with great success.*
>
> *The "concept" is the simple, funny idea that you're writing about. You need to be able to express your concept in a single line or sentence, with as few words as possible. That single line is what I call a "joke." This core comedic concept introduces readers to your writing, so it's often used as the title, headline, or logline for your work.*
>
> *Readers need to know what the concept is before they read your work, and it needs to make them laugh. If the concept makes them laugh, they'll read it. If it doesn't, they won't.*
>
> *Your success in comedy depends on the strength of your concepts.*

You can make use of this book regardless of your skill level or experience. If you're just starting out and you want to be a funnier writer, consider this book your comedy basic training. If you're already a pretty good amateur humor writer but think you could make a career out of it, this book is your comedy college. If you're a successful comedy professional and want to increase your hit ratio, this book is your peak-performance coach.

How to Write Funny explains how comedy works, both in your brain and in the brain of your audience. It outlines the simple tools you've probably already used (if you've ever made anyone laugh on purpose). And it shows how those tools can be sharpened to produce the same effect on command, to create consistently uproarious comedy. It walks you through the dark valley of fear that many of us experience when faced with the prospect of creating comedy, and leads you to a place of quiet confidence. It lays out the master formula for creating funny material seemingly from nothing, whenever you want.

This book focuses on the written word, but its techniques are applicable to all humor media, including stand-up, TV, film, web video, and corporate speaking.

We'll focus on the atom of comedy: the single, one-line joke or funny concept. Learning this elemental particle is a critical first step to success in comedy.

If you have grander aspirations than mere joke writing, like short articles, stories, novels, screenplays or a network TV deal based on your stand-up act, I urge you to be patient. All humor media spring from the written word, and all written comedy springs from the single concept. It's in this microcosm of humor that all the principles of the craft can be learned and honed. Master this fundamental skill, and a much larger comedy world will open up for you like a beautiful flower.

This "concept first" approach is detailed on the opposite page in the first of many Funny-Writing Tips that will dot this book.

One final thought for this Introduction: A lot of people who write books about how to write humor feel pressure to make the book funny. I won't be making any overt attempts. That's not really the point here. If you want to laugh, I suggest you put down this book and pick up any of my other books—or any humor book—and enjoy yourself. If you want a no-nonsense book about how to write humor, read on.

2

YOUR BRAIN'S
COMEDY ENGINE

Writers write. This is one of the first tidbits of advice you get when you start getting serious about writing. And it's good advice. You should be writing. A lot.

But how do you get motivated? Where do you get ideas to write about? And most importantly for our purposes, how do you make your writing funny?

Productive writers of humor churn out a lot of material. They write in a journal, they write in notebooks. They have to write. They're an unstoppable force of nature. If they didn't have jobs as comedy writers, they'd be writing in their spare time. It's how they process what's happening in their lives. It's how they make sense of their world. It's who they are. Naturally, with all that practice, along with some positive reinforcement and guided skill development (if they're lucky), they usually get pretty good at it.

You can, too.

In order to become a successful working writer, you need to get yourself amped up to write as though you have a volcano welling up inside of you that has to blow. I've never met a successful comedy writer who didn't have this essential quality—that of being compelled to write.

To get to that state, you will likely need to solve one of two problems. Each one holds you back from reaching this high level of productivity.

The first is that you're unmotivated. Lack of motivation is usually a symptom of a lack of confidence. When you lack confidence, you don't believe you're going to write anything worthwhile. Worse, you hate everything you write, and can't bear to see it written down. The end result is writer's block. So, you spend a lot of time fretting while staring at a blank sheet of paper or empty screen, producing nothing. Or you clean your desk, pick up around your house, get grout out of your shower stall with a toothbrush—anything besides writing.

> FUNNY-WRITING TIP #2: QUANTITY IS THE KEY TO QUALITY
> *By writing more, you produce a larger pool of raw material to draw quality ideas from. No writer writes only one joke that's pure gold as soon as it's written. One of the myths of writing in general, and comedy writing in particular, is that a genius sits down and cranks out a perfect piece of writing in one draft, without rewriting, editing or proofing. The best comedy writers write dozens and dozens—sometimes hundreds—of jokes, and then carefully select only the best ones to present to readers. They make it seem easy because they never show us all the bad jokes they throw away.*

The second problem is far less common. It's the opposite: you have too much confidence, and love everything you write. You think it's hilarious. However, you can't seem to cull it down to the stuff that will resonate with readers. Your overconfidence renders you immune to any meaningful feedback from the outside world.

Both of these problems are the result of an imbalance in the two key mindsets that a humor writer must learn to balance. A humor writer must be a Clown and an Editor.

The Clown is equivalent to what psychologists used to think of as the right side of the brain: creative, subjective, outside the box, and nonjudgmental. To write humor well, you need to be a Clown. You need to write down every idea you have, no matter how stupid you think it is.

Overconfident writers favor their Clown brain. They love being silly. They'll try anything to get a laugh. They're comedically unrestrained. And while they may not always succeed, they're always "on."

Being a Clown is a big plus if you're a performer. One extremely successful Clown was Jim Carrey in his prime. He was a dynamic performer with a magnetic stage and screen presence. He could say or do just about anything, and the audience loved it because he performed it with unstoppable confidence. Jamie Foxx has a similar quality as a stage performer. He owns the audience, no matter what he's doing.

But when you try to be a Clown on the page, a lot of that confidence and lovable personality that buoyed you in a live-performance medium is lost in translation. Those magical qualities of charisma and presence require in-person delivery. Material that kills on stage comes across as little more than a big mess when put down in the hard light of black-and-white text.

That's exactly what happens when a writer has a Clown-heavy imbalance in the brain.

The Editor is the equivalent of the left side of the brain: logical, objective, organized, and analytical. Most writers are too much of an Editor. Instead of trusting their instincts, they question every choice, and judge every idea before it has a chance to shine. More often than not, they cut every line before they even write it. Nothing is ever perfect enough for the Editor.

To write humor well, you need to be an Editor, but not too much of one. You need to have a reliable system for judging your ideas to make sure they're not drivel, to workshop and finesse the raw material your Clown comes up with, then craft it into superb humor. But if you're too much of an Editor, you'll rarely produce any work.

Just like we need to balance both sides of our brain to function in the world, humor writers need to balance both sides of their comedy brain in order to function as a writer. You need to be a good Clown *and* a good Editor.

DEVELOPING YOUR INNER CLOWN

I recommend two simple exercises to cultivate your inner Clown.

The first exercise is the "Morning Pages." Write for a half hour every day, without stopping, no matter what you're writing—and no matter how bad you think it is. (It doesn't have to be in the morning, but mornings tend to work best for a lot of writers.) This is an extremely helpful habit for writers who tend to be more of an Editor.

proper comedy-brain balance

This exercise comes from Dorothea Brande's schoolmarmish *Becoming a Writer*. Julia Cameron named it in her more user-friendly *The Artist's Way*. Many writers have discovered on their own the astounding results that come from forcing themselves to write for a solid chunk of time every day, without judgment.

You can write about your dreams or your fears, or whatever comes to mind. You can even write, "I don't know what to write," over and over. But eventually you'll want to start spouting some varying thoughts, opinions or ideas. It doesn't matter what they're about. No one's going to see this writing. The important thing is to keep your fingers moving. Don't stop to think, don't stop to correct typos. Just keep writing until the half-hour timer beeps.

Since your focus is humor writing, one tweak I suggest to this exercise is to gently guide your mind to think amusing, funny thoughts while you write. (But it's worth repeating that you still must write without judgment—even if you think what you're writing is terribly unfunny. You must keep writing!) If you find it too difficult to guide yourself toward writing amusing things, that's a valuable discovery. If, when you're in the unconscious "flow" state spurred by this exercise, you tend to write dark, intriguing thoughts instead of funny ones, you may realize that your true calling is to be a mystery writer.

The Morning Pages exercise primes the pump. It forces out material, like a drain-cleaning that clears out all the gunk in your brain so the good stuff can start flowing more easily.

The second exercise: Always keep a little notebook with you. Write down every idea you have, especially ones you find amusing. If you have a thought or make an observation at any point in your day that strikes you as funny, you must write it down. If you have an idea that's not amusing—maybe just an opinion about the world or humanity—write that down, too. These little observations are precious raw material for a comedy writer. They're the crude oil of the funny-writing business. Failing to save them in your notebook is like letting oil from your well spill out all over the sand, costing you thousands—maybe millions—in lost revenue.

Do the Morning Pages exercise every day for a couple of weeks. Make the notebook a part of your lifestyle. If you make a habit of these two simple things, you will go a long way toward rebalancing your brain away from its unproductive Editor and more toward its resource-rich Clown.

Being a Clown is how you generate the raw material you'll use to mold top-notch humor. Most of this raw material is not going to be very good, but don't let that concern you. It's still in its raw form. Keep it all—cherish it—and set it aside to be assessed later when you have your Editor hat on.

Once a week, flip through your notebook and save any ideas you still find amusing. This employs the skills of your Editor. If you find yourself rejecting every idea, you still have some rebalancing to do.

Once you have an idea that you like, be it for something big or small, it's time to put on your Clown hat again and write a first draft. If it's a short joke, write it many times, in different ways, without worrying about whether it's working. If it's a story, crank out a bad first draft. If it's a screenplay or novel, write an unorganized outline. Then put your Editor hat on and assess what you've written. You'll get even better results if you can wait a few days, weeks, or even longer after writing something before you dig it up and put on your Editor hat to assess it. The more you can forget the work of your Clown from days or weeks past, the better your Editor will be at judging it objectively.

If you do this dance between Clown and Editor a few times, you'll improve your dexterity. The back-and-forth reliance on these two very different halves of your brain is like doing mental calisthenics. The more you do it, the more adroit you'll become. Soon you'll be able to move seamlessly between one side and the other as needed, quickly. This is the basic process that a humor writer uses to produce work.

Practice the above regularly, and you'll unleash your inner writer. You'll experience the floodgates of your mind opening wide, and you'll never have writer's block again.

Furthermore, you'll occasionally discover gems within all of your raw source material, wonderfully funny concepts that would have remained forever buried had you not carefully, meticulously sifted through your mind by using this process to find them.

As you can see, developing the Clown side of your brain is not too difficult. Simply practice the exercises above.

DEVELOPING YOUR INNER EDITOR

Developing the Editor side of your brain is much more difficult. It's a more involved and complicated process. If you feel like you're too much of an Editor, you need to not only strengthen your inner Clown, you need to refine your skills as an Editor so that you won't simply slip back into your old pattern of rejecting everything your Clown creates. You need objective criteria for assessing your work sensibly, and you need tools to reshape material so that your Editor is justifiably satisfied with the end result.

If you feel like you're too much of a Clown, you need to develop your inner Editor by learning the same tools and criteria.

Beginning with the next chapter and for the remainder of this book, we'll focus on the specific skills your inner Editor must have at its disposal to create great humor.

CHAPTER 2 ACTION STEPS

1. Buy a little notebook and keep it with you at all times. Write down any thought or observation you have that strikes you as amusing, or even merely interesting.

2. Every day for at least two weeks, do the Morning Pages exercise: Write without stopping for half an hour. Most of what you write in this exercise will be garbage, but you must love and accept it all.

3. At the end of each week, go through your Morning Pages and your notebook. Save any thoughts, ideas, notions or anything amusing to a Shortlist—this is your bank of potential comedy ideas.

THE HUMOR WRITER'S BIGGEST PROBLEM

The biggest problem a humor writer faces—and it's the same problem all writers face—is a practical one that a lot of beginning writers choose to ignore. But it must be confronted, difficult as it is.

This problem is not, "How do I come up with funny ideas?" It's not, "How do I get motivated to write?" You can solve both of these problems by doing the exercises in chapter 2. I'm talking about a much more serious problem. I can help you solve it, and the solution will probably be the most fun you have as a writer, but it's going to be different for everybody, and first, some unpleasant truths must be faced.

Let's say you churn out a few pages of brilliant, funny prose. Then what? Who's going to read it? Your mom, probably. Maybe your best friend. But who else? How are you going to find an audience?

You may think this problem doesn't have anything to do with you or your writing. You may think it's someone else's job to figure it out how to market your work. You may think this problem is largely out of your control, that you just have to sit helplessly and suffer the callous indifference of potential readers, hoping against all odds that your writing gets noticed.

You may plan to post your work online where potentially millions of people will have access to it. Maybe you know about search-engine optimization, and can use those tricks to draw people to your writing.

You may expect that your writing will be published in a high-traffic online or print magazine, then be dutifully promoted on the front page.

You may expect a publisher to buy your book, then promote it with advertising and a book tour, sending you to various cities to do book signings and appear on TV shows.

Let's be realistic. Even if your goals are modest, and you plan to post your work online, do you know how many blogs there are? How about websites and Twitter feeds? There's more writing published online every day than has ever been published in the history of human civilization. With millions more people going online every day, that number probably doubles every few weeks. The sheer volume of writing available to modern reader is unfathomable. And it's safe to assume that all of this writing is using SEO, link exchanging, or even paid advertising to find readers. Anyone trying to publish writing online is so far behind before even starting, it's enough to make you want to give up.

If you're lucky enough to have your humor piece published by one of the tiny handful of name-brand magazines that still buy unsolicited humor, you'll need to make sure your writing is sharp enough that it stands out among the other stories in the magazine—all of which are professionally calculated to compete for readers' limited time and even more limited attention. This is to say nothing of standing out among the stories in the stacks of hundreds of other magazines released every month.

If a publisher sends you on a tour and books you on TV, you have enjoyed a privilege afforded only the most established and successful writers, and even they—every one of them—would, if you pressed them, complain that their publisher doesn't promote their work nearly enough.

There's no magic marketing spell that the Internet or a publisher can put on your writing that will make readers read it.

This problem is compounded by the fact that readers are a rare thing. Most people don't like to read. They'd rather do just about anything else. In our culture of easy entertainment and instant gratification, reading is akin to homework in most people's minds.

Have you ever noticed how newspapers and magazines list the box-office receipts for movies in the millions of dollars? They also list TV ratings, showing how many millions of households tuned into the most popular shows. By contrast, have you ever noticed that they don't list how many books were sold every week, or how much money those books made? Books are treated differently, and with good reason. Bestseller lists like Amazon and *The New York Times* rank books in order of which ones sold the most. But that only tells part of the story. Where's the money, like in the TV and movie rankings?

They don't tell you the dollar figures because the numbers would be embarrassing. In some weeks, a book only needs to sell a few hundred copies in order to make it onto the bestseller list. So, in comparison to the number-one movie of the week, which may have grossed $40 million, the number-one book might have grossed $4,000.

So, the big problem remains: How are you going to get people to read your work? If you don't solve this problem, you'll never find an audience, and your hope of being a working humor writer will be crushed.

Okay, that's enough grim reality! On to the fun solution to this problem. Getting ahead of this problem is in many ways what the craft of writing is all about, and it will super-charge the quality of your writing if you can boldly face this important challenge.

The good news is, this solution is well within your control. It's not someone else's problem. It's your responsibility to find readers, and there are tricks you can employ to get yourself noticed among the sea of other writing in the world. In fact, you can become a popular humor writer by turning this most difficult problem into your greatest advantage.

Don't wait for readers to find you. Make yourself easy to find. The first and most important step to making yourself easy to find is to make your writing accessible. That is, make it understandable to the widest possible audience, appealing to them with as universal a message as possible. Also, present it in a format or medium that readers have easy access to.

By pushing the limits of accessibility, you will virtually compel readers to read your writing. It will jump off the page or screen, grab them, and force them to read it.

There's a thing I used to do when reading the Sunday comics. I never liked *Garfield*. I thought it was one of the worst comic strips in the newspaper. But it was so economically written that even as my eyes passed by it on the way to looking at another comic strip (one that I actually wanted to read), I would read it involuntarily! Jim Davis, the strip's writer, demonstrates an extremely effective first salvo in the quest for accessibility: make it short. Brevity, as we've heard, is the soul of wit. Brevity is also the soul of accessibility, which is arguably just as important as wit.

FUNNY-WRITING TIP #3: MAKE IT ACCESSIBLE
Accessible writing is easy to find and easy to read. It's made available to as many readers as possible, written clearly and simply to appeal to as many readers as possible, and covers subject matter that's understandable (ideally of great interest) to as many readers as possible. Because the audience for the written word is so small, it's important to increase the size of your potential audience every way you can. Reading is hard enough work as it is. Don't make readers work even harder to find or understand your writing. When assessing any humorous concept you've written, you need to ask yourself, How accessible is it?

Let's look at other ways to solve the problem of how to get people to read your writing. All is fair in love, war and writing. You can break any rule you want in order to get readers. And the first thing you're going to want to do is steal. That's right, steal.

To be very clear, I'm not talking about stealing other people's jokes. If you do that, you may get a laugh, but you'll lose the respect of any readers who recognize your theft, and you'll lose the respect of your peers—especially the peer you stole from—and you'll have a very difficult time ever shaking the reputation within the comedy-writing community as someone who steals jokes.

Don't ever steal anyone's jokes, and don't ever plagiarize anyone's writing.

What I'm recommending is stealing some of the attention-getting traits of other humor media. This is a secret trick used by some of the most successful humor writers to get their writing noticed.

Just as a plant needs to come up with creative ways to attract bees to pollinate it, your writing needs you to think of creative ways to attract readers. The prettiest, most fragrant flower is going to attract the most bees.

To do this, we first need to lay out the other media and determine their specific traits.

THE SEVEN HUMOR MEDIA

There are seven media for humor: prose, TV/web video, movies, audio/podcast, stage, visual (image only, no words), and street art (performance art for unsuspecting audiences, such as pranks, flash mobs, graffiti and outdoor advertising).

We've already laid out one of the biggest weaknesses of the prose medium (print or web, text only): it's not very popular. But let's take stock of its strengths.

Prose has your audience's undivided attention. This is not true of the other media, whose audiences can (and often do) exercise, wash dishes, have a conversation, or check their messages while they're consuming the entertainment. They can get distracted by just about anything. Not so with prose. If they're reading your work, they're not paying attention to anything else.

Another great strength of prose is its intimacy. Prose gets inside the mind of your audience, weaving your ideas with theirs to create a unique and highly personal world in their imagination. Your work comes to life for them in a way that's unattainable by any other media. Readers take ownership of this "word picture" because they helped create it. Radio drama is the only other medium that rivals this magical strength, but radio drama is, sadly, a dead art. No one produces it anymore, and audiences have forgotten how to listen to it. So, there's no danger of the written word facing competition from radio drama any time soon, unless audiences start digging up 1950s episodes of *Suspense* or *Gunsmoke* in droves, which is extremely unlikely.

One great strength of prose is that it lasts longer than any of the other media—a lot longer. We're still reading great works of humor written by Mark Twain in the late 1800s. Jonathan Swift's *Gulliver's Travels* (written in 1726) was recently made into a movie starring Jack Black. We're still getting laughs from the humor writing of Shakespeare, Chaucer, even Aristophanes, whose writing dates back 2400 years. In any other medium, you can't go back more than a quarter century without the entertainment appearing hopelessly out of date in terms of production quality alone. You can only go back a few years with movies or TV shows before a lot of modern audiences will tune out. Most people nowadays won't tolerate standard definition, mono sound, and certainly not black-and-white movies or old TV-show kinescopes with scratchy sound, as brilliant as some of those shows may be.

Great humor writing—especially Satire, which is the kind we're going to focus on in this book—is universal. It can transcend time, fashion and taste, rising from centuries past to become just as timely and meaningful as the day it was written.

But these strengths alone don't make up for prose's weaknesses. Its potential audience is still tiny, and it's perceived as impersonal and intellectual. It's just a bunch of black-and-white symbols that feel like a chore to read—not exactly what most jaded modern audiences would consider a good time, or "must see" entertainment.

Let's look to some of the other media to see what strengths we might appropriate, in order to give our prose a needed boost.

relative popularity of the 7 humor media

movies

TV/web video

audio/podcast
stage
visual
street art
prose

Comic strips have already shown us the importance of brevity. Another great attribute of comic strips is their use of the visual medium. Comic strips are, after all, a mixed medium (a combination of prose and visual). Draw a little picture next to your writing, as I've done throughout my career (and throughout this book), or include a funny photo or any other kind of image that illustrates your message. This simple addition can make the writing next to it exponentially more appealing to readers, and therefore a lot more accessible.

Internet memes use this tactic to great effect, combining catchy images with very brief text to generate potentially massive popularity, or at least awareness of their writing.

One of the late 20th century's greatest satirists, Matt Groening, got his start using the visual medium. He was a writer who, even though he couldn't draw very well, decided to draw pictures next to his writing to make it more appealing, turning it into a comic strip ("Life in Hell"), which led to an opportunity to create *The Simpsons.*

TV/web video is the world's most accessible and therefore most popular medium. This is one of its strengths. People love it. We're addicted to it. It's actually difficult to avoid consuming humor in this medium. It's thrust at us from our computers, our phones, in taxicabs, elevators and gas stations. And a lot of people leave the TV on in their homes all day.

The TV/web-video medium has weaknesses, too. It's expensive to produce, and it takes a lot of labor from a lot of different skillsets.

However, a words-only web video is relatively inexpensive to produce. Add some music, and you've got an excellent way to distribute your writing that makes use of the considerable strengths of the TV/web-video medium. A lot of YouTube videos employ this tactic. We used it at *The Onion* to launch our web-video spin-off, *ONN*, in the mid-2000s. Our introductory teaser trailer for *ONN* featured little more than a few words set to music. The web videos that followed featured on-screen prose humor like segment titles, lower thirds, and a moving headline crawl. This co-opting of the video medium brought a lot of readers to theonion.com to read our prose.

The audio/podcast medium is alive and well, despite the fact that radio drama (a subset) is dead. Audio/podcast is the next most intimate medium, after prose. It's also a uniquely accessible medium. People listen to podcasts and audiobooks on their way to work, while running on their treadmills, and anywhere else they want. Podcasts are a great promotional medium writers can use to make potential readers aware of their writing.

Writing a script for a podcast is another great way to reach audiences. All of those podcasters have to get material from somewhere.

One strength shared by just about every other medium besides prose is the human element. These media usually do best when a live person presents the written material, either as dialog or monologue. It's impossible to calculate how much more energized an audience becomes when they're being entertained by a person as opposed to a bunch of stifling words. They love it.

The stage medium taps into the power of the human connection better than any other media. When you're sitting in a theater just a few feet or a few yards from the performer, you'll find the writing recited by this performer far more engaging than any you'll ever see on TV, in a movie, or certainly on the printed page.

You can give the human touch to your writing by creating a facade. When the words become a curtain, and there's a personality behind that curtain, your writing is suddenly electrified as if it's a live performance. Your reader senses the intelligence behind the curtain and the writing comes alive in a way that it can't when you write "on the nose" (the term for writing exactly what you think). There's much more detail on how to achieve this effect in chapter 6.

Street art is one of my favorite media. Audiences who get entertained on the street when they're not expecting it are the best audiences. They're delighted by the surprise inherent in the presentation. There are countless legal ways to get your writing in front of readers using this medium.

The Onion began as a newspaper that was dispensed free on the street. So, part of its early appeal came from using the street-art medium. This was, in fact, the primary medium used by *The Onion* to introduce itself to new readers in its formative years. People would walk past grocery stores or bars where free weekly newspapers are distributed, and they'd see *The Onion* among the offerings. At first, they'd be confused by it—the outlandish headlines were out of place among the straight-laced alternative news, music, or LGBT weeklies that were often found in the same areas. Once passersby realized *The Onion* was a humor publication, they fell in love with it immediately. To this day I hear people fondly reminisce about their first discovery of *The Onion* on the streets of Madison, Denver, San Francisco, or one of the other cities where *The Onion* was distributed in its early years, and how absolutely delighted they were to find humor in such an unexpected place.

That kind of surprise and delight is one of the greatest strengths of the street-art medium. It's virtually impossible to achieve that level of surprise in any of the other media. In all other media, the audience is, at least on some level, expecting to be entertained, which necessarily diminishes the amount of surprise or discovery they can experience.

Carol Kolb is a brilliant TV writer who got her start at *The Onion* in Madison, ultimately rising to the rank of editor-in-chief in the early 2000s. She got noticed and initially hired by *The Onion* largely due to her hilarious street art.

After a college student had gone missing under dubious circumstances, flyers were posted all over campus, asking, "Have you seen this woman?" next to a photocopy of the student's picture. Kolb produced her own flyer and posted it all over campus, asking, "Have you seen this man?" next to a photocopy of Al from the TV show *Happy Days*. It was a bold and edgy parody that pierced straight through the media clutter to make a lot of unsuspecting readers laugh.

How can you get your writing seen in unusual or creative ways? What rules of the prose medium can you break in order to ring out above the competition and get noticed? What tactic can you borrow from the more popular or the more fringe media to give your writing as much of a boost as possible?

TIMING

We've all heard how important timing is to joke-telling. But how do you explain the success of written comedy when, as a prose writer, you have virtually no control over timing? You don't dictate when the reader reads your humor, how fast they read it, or in what order. In all aspects it seems, time itself—and therefore timing—is removed from the equation.

And how do you learn timing? This is one of those aspects of the craft of comedy that many people believe can't be taught. I agree it's very difficult for a book or any kind of "how to" comedy instruction to impart ideal timing in performance (or any medium other than prose). However, I believe it is absolutely learnable. A book like this can get you started, but ultimately timing in performance is a skill that can only be mastered through practice. If you practice being funny in person and on stage with dedication (that means trying, failing, and repeating), in time, you'll learn it. It may take years, but you'll learn it.

Timing in prose, however, is easier to learn, and you can learn it faster, because there are certain best practices.

> FUNNY-WRITING TIP #4: MAKE IT SHORT
>
> *Anything worth saying is worth saying briefly. It may take more time (Mark Twain famously apologized for a letter's lengthiness by explaining that he didn't have time to make it short), but this is time well spent. Sometimes cutting a word or two can make a line twice as funny, or turn an unfunny line into a funny one. Experiment with your work by cutting words. See if anything's lost. And use simpler, shorter words when possible. By trimming your writing, you force yourself to get at the heart of what you have to say, and you'll say it in a way that readers can more easily digest.*

It's true that time is largely removed from the equation in prose, but there are tiny fulcrums to be found, and when each is leveraged for maximum gain, prose timing can be surprisingly effective. Here are the primary timing elements, however small, you do in fact control in prose:

- *when you release your writing*
- *how quickly or how slowly you pace it*
- *the order in which you present your jokes*
- *the type size (making the part you want your audience to read first biggest, and making the part you want them to read last smallest, for example)*
- *where and how you break your paragraphs*
- *the use of bullet points for emphasis*

- *the use of photo captions, pull quotes, headlines, and other ways to partition jokes*

Play with these elements to maximize the impact of your prose. While there's no guarantee that your audience will follow your breadcrumbs exactly as you intend, the good news is that readers welcome any such handholding you offer. It makes them feel like they are in the hands of a professional writer, which makes your comedy writing more accessible and therefore gives it the best chance of being perceived as funny.

I offer a few other Funny-Writing Tips throughout this book to maximize your timing leverage within individual jokes, such as Tip #4: ("Make It Short," page 39), Tip #8: ("Put the Funny Part Last," page 58).

Controlling your readers' experience and exactly how they consume your work is, in many ways, the single most important key to making longer-form comedy writing work. But we're getting ahead of ourselves. I go into the power of Context in much more detail in the second book in this series, *How to Write Funnier*. For now, let's continue with the basics.

CHAPTER 3 ACTION STEPS

1. Write a list of some of the strengths and weaknesses of prose compared to the strengths and weaknesses of the other six media.

2. Make a list of ideas for overcoming the weaknesses of the prose medium in your own writing. What are some strengths of other media that you could employ to help readers find your work?

3. Come up with 10 ideas for getting your writing in front of readers faces in ways that would be incredibly fun for both you and them.
4. Write 10 short jokes, short enough to be a "one-liner," or about 5–10 words. To get ideas for your jokes, look through your notebook, Morning Pages, or Shortlist, or just try come up with ideas off the top of your head. If you've

never done this before, it may be a strange or even painful experience. None-theless, it's a threshold you must cross if you want to learn how to write funny. Rest assured more tools are coming in successive chapters to make the process easier, but first you have to jump in the water.

4

HOW TO GET LAUGHS

Humor is the magic ingredient that makes a dull life fascinating, a sad life happy, and an empty life fulfilling. It's a ray of sunshine in a cold and unforgiving universe—the light at the end of the tunnel of the human condition. Those lucky few who can find humor in a situation—any situation—will not only endure it, but enjoy it, and inspire others to do the same.

Studies show that people who have a hardy sense of humor have more friends, make more money, and live longer.

No less than the American Cancer Society promotes the power of "humor therapy." Doctors endorse similar treatments for chronic pain sufferers. Laughter Yoga, the practice of fake-laughing until it becomes real laughing, stimulates deep breathing and leads to physical and mental rejuvenation, even demonstrable healing.

Humor, along with its primary effect, laughter, is a big deal. It's important to us all. You ought to be commended for wanting to make the world a better place by working to improve your ability to make people laugh.

But what makes people laugh, really? Not fake-laugh, but genuinely laugh. You need to be able to answer this question if you're to succeed at making them laugh. There are different kinds of laughs, and they vary in quality and desirability.

Over 90 percent of all spontaneously generated laughter is nervous laughter. It's people trying to grease the wheels of a conversation or break some tension, real or perceived. There's nothing actually funny going on with this kind of laughter. There's no comedy being crafted. This kind of laughter, though ubiquitous, is an empty, non-healing kind. If laughter is food for the soul, this is the McDonald's of laughter.

World-Instances-of-laughter breakdown

social anxiety: 90%

Spontaneous funny occurence: 9%

crafted comedy : <1%

crafted prose comedy : ~.00001%

Roughly 9 percent of all laughter is good, pure, hardy laughter in response to real-life situations—that crazy thing the dog just did, or the non-injurious fall Myrtle just had off the trampoline. This is the kind of laughter that's good for your lungs, releases endorphins, and generally makes life fun. The more you can get of this kind of laughter, the better off you'll be. Problem is, these kinds of laughs are very difficult to engineer. They almost always happen by accident.

The remaining 1 percent of laughter is the most rare. It's laughter gold: an involuntary response not to a real-life situation, but to something that was consciously crafted for the purpose of generating laughs. The overwhelming majority of this 1 percent of all laughter is brought on by stage, TV/web video, movie or audio/podcast entertainment. This laughter is often mild, or offered in artificially enhanced form either willingly or by producers' careful manipulation.

When someone is performing for us on the stage, we laugh, even if we don't think it's very funny. There's a social contract at work in these situations. If we feel like laughing a little, we might subconsciously exaggerate our response to appease a performer or join in with a laughing crowd. We might also consciously exaggerate our laughter if we're at the taping of a TV comedy show and the producers have spent as much as an hour prior to showtime encouraging us to laugh often and loudly.

Hearing other people laugh entices us to laugh more readily. Producers of TV shows take great pains to record live audience laughter because they understand its power. The sound of this laughter activates the social contract in us even if we aren't a part of that original audience, but are watching the show long after the taping, alone at home. Producers also occasionally add canned laughter to a show's soundtrack, either to enhance existing laughs deemed too lackluster to do the job, or to create the illusion of a live audience where none exists. (Canned laughter is audience laughter pieced together from previous performances and then applied to a different performance.) Canned laughter is meant to trigger the social contract artificially, encouraging at-home laughs in those not yet inured to the effects of such cheesy tactics.

Roughly .00001% of all laughter remains. This tiny sliver of laughter is generated by nothing but the written word, no interpersonal reaction with friends or family, no performer, no personal connection, no music, no editing, no sound effects, no laugh track—nothing to enhance the experience beyond a string of words on a page or screen.

Starting in this chapter, I'm going to dissect what type of humor will result in the kind of big, hardy laughs that are the most healing—the milk-coming-out-of-your-nose kinds of laughs—using only the written word.

We'll unlock these tactics first by uncovering the one thing you're absolutely going to need, the one essential ingredient in all humor, without which humor cannot take place.

There are many things that are helpful in humor, like relatability, truth, timing, tragedy, or the breaking of taboos. But humor can still exist without these things. There's only one thing absolutely required for humor to exist, and that is surprise. Even when something expected or even downright predictable happens that makes us laugh, that predictable event must unfold in a surprising way in order to be funny.

So, how do you get laughs? Surprise people.

Of course, not all surprise is funny. Some surprise is scary, some shocking. Some annoying. It's the particular kinds of surprises that make people laugh that we'll be focusing on in this book.

CLICHÉ-BUSTING

Because surprise is the core element of all humor, clichés must be avoided in all humor writing. This is perhaps the most important single thing you can do to instantly elevate your writing to a funnier level.

In Strunk and White's *The Elements of Style*, the seminal book on how to write competently, the authors offer as a basic writing tip the simple but effective advice, "avoid clichés like the plague." They include a cliché in the advice so there's no mistaking what we're talking about. It's a good idea to avoid using common phrases like "like the plague," "that's neither here nor there," or "six of one, half dozen of the other," or other useful, very clever phrases in any kind of writing. In prose, these clichés, and thousands more like them, shouldn't be used because they were originally made up by the witty writer or conversationalist who first used them.

At first, these phrases are fun. But when used over and over, they become clichés, and after a time they annoy more than they amuse. The cliché user is admitting failure by using them. The message is, "I can't think of a more clever or useful phrase, so I'm just going to steal a clever phrase that someone else wrote a long time ago." Because clichés are common, using them doesn't feel like stealing to most writers. In fact, using clichés is one of the laziest and most unoriginal things you can do as a writer.

Good writing is creative. Good writers dream up new ways to say things.

Avoiding clichés is especially important in humor writing. In humor writing, clichés are not defined necessarily as clever phrases you didn't invent. In some cases you may *want* to use clichéd phrases in a joke in order to communicate a funny idea in a relatable way. In humor writing, the clichés to avoid are jokes we've heard before, topics that have been joked about enough, or patterns of humor that have been overused. Humor clichés tend to evolve as old ones are quietly retired from common use and new ones emerge. Here's a short list of just a few examples that have stood the test of time as of this writing:

- *The poor quality of airline food*
- *"I could tell you, but then I'd have to kill you."*
- *"That's what she said."*
- *Big fake laugh that devolves into an unimpressed groan.*
- *Illustrating how white people and black people talk differently*
- *"You should see the other guy" (when someone is roughed up)*
- *The taint*
- *"I just threw up in my mouth a little bit."*
- *California "Surfer dude" character*
- *TV character bad-mouths someone, not realizing that someone is right behind them*

For a complete and continually updated list of the most common clichés in comedy, go to www.howtowritefunny.com/list.

FUNNY-WRITING TIP #5: AVOID CLICHÉS

If you've heard a joke or funny phrase before, don't repeat it. It's also a good idea to avoid subject matter that's been joked about endlessly, like how men hog the remote control, airline food is bad, or white people can't jump. These are comedy clichés. Look at every aspect of your comedy writing and ask yourself honestly, "Is this original?" If you can't answer yes, you're probably using clichés.

Clichés like these ring like a discordant note in the ear of the sophisticated reader of humor. If you use a clichéd joke, topic or character, your reader will immediately and instinctively know that your humor writing is not very good, and they probably won't stick with it for very long.

One of the surest ways to tell an amateur humor writer from a professional humor writer is that the amateur will use a lot of clichés, and the professional won't. Professionals come up with their own jokes, explore fresh ways of phrasing ideas. They're always searching for a new approach or a new angle that's never been written before.

There's no surprise with clichés because we've seen the jokes before. Only fresh ideas, unique perspectives or original thoughts can surprise. Consequently, only fresh, unique and original writing can get laughs. Well, clichés might get laughs from those who've never heard them before, but you don't want those kinds of laughs. This may seem like contradictory advice, given that the goal in humor writing is maximum accessibility, but getting laughs only from the lowest common denominator limits your accessibility in two ways. First, unsophisticated audiences will laugh at a lot of things that sophisticated audiences won't, which means the humor may be accessible to the unsophisticated, but it's a turn-off for the sophisticated. You create accessible humor by appealing to the widest possible audience, lowbrow and highbrow alike. Second, there's no reason to use clichés to appeal to unsophisticated audiences when so many other, legitimate tools work just as well.

CATEGORIES OF PROSE HUMOR

Written humor comes in five distinct categories. Understanding the difference between these categories can help you get clear about your own writing, and where it naturally falls in the spectrum. Only one of these categories provides the maximum potential for generating surprise, and the laughs that follow. It also offers the largest possible audience.

These categories exist in a range from the basic to the sophisticated. At the basic end of the range, the humor is simple, and has more narrow appeal. At the other end, the humor is more layered, and has more broad appeal—it also takes more skill to produce.

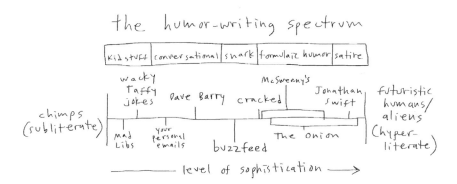

Just like visible light and audible sound exist on a spectrum, beyond which humans can't see or hear, humor also has a spectrum. And just like light and sound have a small range within their perceptible spectrums that produce an effect that's most pleasing to the senses (for example, a sound of 50 Hz is audible, but not very pleasant—just a low rumbling sound without much definition—but a layered, harmonic sound of 440 Hz, with high-frequency overtones and rich undertones, can be a beautiful note of music), humor produced at the highest end of the spectrum with overtones and undertones that resonate across the entire perceptible spectrum of humor will produce the most hilarious comedy.

Written humor that's too far outside the sophisticated end of the spectrum on the right, or too far beyond the basic end on the left, won't make very many people laugh. It will either confound anyone but unimaginably intelligent aliens or futuristic humans on the right, or fail to impress anyone but chimps on the left. But when we produce humor somewhere within this spectrum, we have a fighting chance of making a lot of actual people laugh.

On the bottom end of the spectrum is Kid Stuff. These are the literary equivalent of a funny face, a pratfall, or other very basic types of humor that appeal to the less-than-intellectual reader. There's no higher calling here, no complex structures. This end of the spectrum is made up of things like basic discordance, incongruity, and other elements of surprise based on a very limited understanding of the world. When you call a tree a "dog," for example, or when you pretend to be confused and call a child by the wrong name, or ascribe the wrong age to a child, most 3- to 5-year-olds will find this hilarious. Read any *Sesame Street* book for very young kids to find good examples of this kind of humor. Kid Stuff isn't likely to tickle the funny bones of too many adult readers.

On the upper end of the Kid Stuff category is simple pun-based jokes from joke books, the jokes on Wacky Taffy packages, as well as simple forms of societal-norm-defying Madcap or Shock-based humor like you might see in *Mad* Magazine or the now-defunct *Nick* magazine, forms of humor we'll dig into in more detail in later chapters.

However, as unsophisticated as Kid Stuff may be, these simple things that make a young kid laugh contain the seeds from which more sophisticated humor is derived.

Next on the spectrum is the Conversational category. This is prose that's written with the author's personality laid bare, or "on the nose," with no attempt to disguise opinions or ideas through another voice or literary device. There is a character here; the inherent character of the writer, but it's not a comedic construct like a character you might find in more advanced humor writing. It's merely the real personality of the writer. This is the type of writing you might see in personal letters or notes, where writers attempt to play off their natural personalities, or key character traits they're known for. Dave Barry is probably the most famous purveyor of this kind of writing. David Sedaris is another, though Sedaris uses more sophisticated story structure, veering out of purely comedic structure and into the realm of dramatic writing.

Very close to Conversational but slightly more sophisticated is Snark. It's a ubiquitous kind of humor writing most commonly found on blogs, magazines that are trying to sound hip, Facebook posts, and a lot of other places, too. Entertainment and sports-news writing often aspires to this style. Extremely popular now, Snark is essentially Conversational, but with the added layer of smart-alecky sarcasm, the wry attitude of someone who's plugged into the most desirable trends. It's the classic character archetype of the Know-It-All, but in a transparent form. The veneer of Snark is a literary device that masks the writer, but not very believably. As we will see, concealing the writer and the writer's true intent—and doing so believably—is one of the secrets to good humor writing.

Snark is identifiable for its brazen use of clichés borrowed from other Snark writing. Clichés, almost more than the too-hip attitude, are what define this style of writing. Like other humor clichés, those of Snark are cyclical, but as of this writing, "Best. [Insert a thing]. Ever." (with periods between each word) is enjoying widespread use. Faux-Conversational words and phrases like "Welp," (as a version of "Well") "I know, right?," "Ya think?," "Hells no," and "Wow. Just wow," imply a conversation with the reader that's not happening.

Acronyms like LOL, LMFAO and IMHO are all the spawn of Snark. Intentionally misspeaking, using phrases like "the webs," or "bad maths," have become popular since George W. Bush's famous utterance of "the Internets" during a debate with John Kerry.

There are too many other clichés to list, and new ones are always forming. Writers of Snark use these clichés with impugnity because they're an integral part of the style. That said, Snark can be effective (and funny) when done well and without clichés. Mike Nelson (of *Mystery Science*

Theater 3000 fame) has written some very funny essays and books in this style. John Hodgman and Sarah Vowell use the form skillfully, though a lot of their writing hits more sophisticated notes as well

One of the problems with Snark nowadays is that it's overused, and therefore writers in this category have difficulty standing out from the crowd.

The likely origin of the modern Snark voice is the great but short-lived *Spy* magazine. *Spy* featured some of the best humor writing ever produced in America. But writers today attempting to copy *Spy*'s snarky style (or, more likely, copy a copy of *Spy*'s snarky style) forget that *Spy* never used clichés.

FUNNY-WRITING TIP #6: PROOFREAD

Get your spelling, grammar and syntax right. It's not that hard. Make a solid effort to ensure no typos slip through. For a really important piece of work like a submission for a job, get some help proofreading. Your work might be just as funny as the competition's, but if you have a few misspellings and bad punctuation and they don't, guess who will get the job.

The next category on the spectrum is Formulaic Humor. Here multiple layers of humor are employed, and the primary tools of comedy (the 11 Funny Filters, covered in chapter 6) are used skillfully to elicit laughter. That's the formula. Formulaic Humor is typically written by professional comedy writers.

Formulaic Humor is often not in a first-person voice, but assumes other character voices and formats. The writer is no longer the focus, like in Conversational or Snark. Rest assured the writer is driving the bus, but entertaining diversions are placed between the reader and the writer in order to conceal the writer and achieve laughs through any number of comedic facades, things like made-up characters, a parody context and others—all of which will be covered in great detail later in this book.

National Lampoon was a standout in Formulaic Humor until its decline in the late 1970s, as have Garrison Keillor, *The New Yorker*'s "Shouts & Murmurs" column, and *Spy* Magazine. The extremely short-lived *Army Man* (finally online at armymans.tumblr.com), was a textbook example.

Formulaic Humor is most often seen on TV and in movies. In these media, the facade of Character is built in, which instantly creates a face that the reader can relate to. It also puts some distance between the writer and the audience, which makes for far more engaging writing.

COMEDIC STRUCTURE VS. DRAMATIC STRUCTURE

Comedic structure entails establishing and then escalating a single joke. This simple structure is found in online comedy articles, jokes, one-liners, and TV/web video or movie sketches lasting no more than 5–10 minutes. Comedic structure can produce some extremely funny short entertainment. But if a humor writer wants to write something longer, like a short story, novella, novel, or screenplay, comedic structure can no longer be used.

It's impossible to tell a compelling, longer-form story in which the primary structure is comedic. Comedic structure falls apart after only a couple of pages or 5–10 minutes. Audiences get bored with it. Only dramatic story structure can sustain audience interest beyond that time frame. Therefore, in a longer work, telling a story becomes the primary goal. Getting laughs becomes secondary.

This is why even in goofy Adam Sandler movies there has to be a semi-realistic love-interest storyline, and a moment of genuine pathos for the main character at the end of Act II. (The only time you see purely comedic structure in a feature film is in sketch movies.)

Learning how to structure comedic stories using dramatic story structure is outside the scope of this book. If you want to write funny stories using dramatic structure, learn the comedy-writing tools outlined in this book first. You'll then find it easier to infuse your longer-form stories with humor. See the second book in this series, How to Write Funnier, *for more on dramatic structure in comedy.*

The high standard of Formulaic Humor sometimes causes it to pop into the next highest category on the spectrum, as is the case with all the publications mentioned above.

The top category on the humor writing spectrum is Satire. Satire is writing that employs all the tools and techniques from the other categories, most notably Formulaic Humor, but it offers something extra on top. Like Formulaic Humor, Satire is adept at getting laughs, but it has one additional, hidden feature that the other categories lack. This secret ingredient is the one thing that nudges humor writing out of any lower category and into the Satire category. It's because of this secret ingredient that the laughs Satire can generate are a lot more satisfying and memorable.

Writing in any category can occasionally achieve a level of Satire (like Dr. Seuss in Kid Stuff or David Sedaris in Conversational). Those who consistently achieve the satirical category in short articles are *The Onion*, and occasional writers for *The New Yorker*'s "Shouts and Murmurs" column, like Ian Frazier, Andy Borowitz and Ben Greenman. In books, Satire's masters are Kurt Vonnegut, Leonard Wibberley, Mark Twain, Jonathan Swift, and other luminaries of Satire dating back to ancient Greece and Rome. One standout genius who only published one novel (posthumously) is John Kennedy Toole, whose *Confederacy of Dunces* is a masterpiece of English Satire. However, these books all employ dramatic structure. Purely comedically structured satirical books include *The Onion*'s *Our Dumb Century, The Daily Show*'s *America: The Book, and* John Hodgman's *The Areas of My Expertise*.

Outside of the prose media, many writers operate in the Satire category, most notably the writers of *The Daily Show* and its spin-offs, of course. *The Simpsons, Seinfeld*, and classic TV shows like *All In The Family* are satirical as well, but they also employ tools of dramatic structure. *Monty Python's Flying Circus* is the supreme example of modern, purely comedically structured satirical TV writing.

Satirical humor has the potential to appeal to all levels of readers. It freely uses Kid Stuff to appeal to the least sophisticated audiences, but also employs a layer of intelligence to appeal to the most sophisticated audiences. This broad appeal gives it the best chance of any category to connect with the largest possible audience.

In the next chapter, we'll delve into Satire's secret ingredient, and spell out how you can use this ingredient in your own writing.

> FUNNY-WRITING TIP #7: HAVE SOMETHING TO SAY
>
> *To be a writer, the first thing you need is something to say—something you feel strongly about. Without that, why are you writing? To find something to say, go through your notebook and Morning Pages once a week. In time, you'll find volumes of topics that not only fire your passions, but that others will find interesting as well.*

CHAPTER 4 ACTION STEPS

1. In your next Morning Pages exercise, try ruminating on these questions: What kind of laughs do you want your writing to elicit? What category has your writing habitually been in? Do you tend to use clichés?

2. Write 10 one-sentence jokes using no clichés.

THE SECRET INGREDIENT

Given that surprise is the one element that all humor requires, let's look at how we can generate it in prose.

We've learned ways to engineer surprise by borrowing strengths from other media. You can add a surprising image to your writing to draw readers in. You can pair your writing with a video in order to take advantage of timing. You can write through the voice of a character, conjuring the human connection that makes media like stage, TV and movies so engaging.

These tactics can be effective for initially drawing a reader into your writing. Using a character voice, especially, can command a reader's attention. However, once they get the joke, or understand what's supposed to be funny about it, they may tire of the writing and abandon it if there's nothing deeper going on.

Using only comedic structure, you can keep the surprises coming and create the feeling that the writing is getting funnier and funnier through the use of Satire's secret ingredient.

Satire has something to say—something important—that's hidden in the literal text. In the other categories, humor itself is the end goal. Just like the writers of Formulaic Humor and other categories, the satirist uses expertly crafted humor calculated to make readers laugh uproariously, but does so as a means to an end. Yes, readers are laughing at Satire, but they're also getting this secret message. This message makes the material funnier, the laughs more satisfying. Some unsophisticated readers may not even notice the message, or may not care. It doesn't matter. They're still laughing.

We call this hidden message Subtext.

In any sophisticated writing, there's more there than just the literal words on the page. There's something else that those words aren't saying, but rest assured it's being communicated clearly to any reasonably intelligent reader. What's being communicated is the Subtext.

> **Funny-Writing Tip #8: Put the Funny Part Last**
> *A joke usually works best when the funniest or most unexpected word or detail in it comes last. Often, when you're assessing whether a joke works, you might notice the funny part is at the beginning or the middle. Try moving it as close to the end as possible. That can make your line funnier simply by delaying the surprise.*

When you read a joke, or a funny line in a larger story, you add two and two in your mind, and you expose the Subtext that the writer has hidden in the joke. It's this exposure that surprises you and causes you to laugh.

In a joke, the Subtext is what you "get." If you didn't get a joke, it means you couldn't decipher the Subtext. If you got the joke, and laughed, you were able to uncover the joke's Subtext subconsciously, exactly as the writer intended.

All good jokes have Subtext, as do all good comedy articles, short stories and novels. But in the less-sophisticated humor categories, the Subtext has nothing to say. It may reveal that a word has two meanings, reveal a character trait, or tell a backstory, but there's no meaningful message.

What makes the Subtext of Satire special is the quality of its message.

Subtext in Satire is a value judgment or opinion held by the writer. In the best satirical writing, the Subtext is universal, something that just about anyone can relate to. In the very best writing, it points out something wrong with the world, a fatal flaw or weakness in humanity or the universe. It can even be a sad fact, something that cannot be changed, yet the writer is compelled to point it out, to yearn publicly for things to be different.

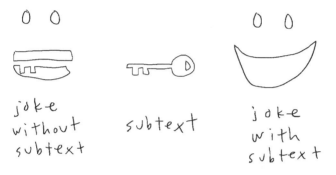

The funniest humor often has the most interesting, original and astute Subtext. A joke can still be funny with mediocre Subtext, but rich, interesting Subtext will almost always make it better.

Subtext isn't the same as a theme or moral. The theme of a piece of writing is the general subject being explored, and it often can't be reduced to a single statement. Subtext, on the other hand, can be. Theme is often overtly articulated in the writing. In certain screenplay-writing circles, for example, writers are told to be sure a secondary character verbally states the movie's theme on a certain page in every script. Morals are similar. A parable or other type of lesson ends with "the moral of the story," which is advice the writer would like readers to learn from the story and live by. Subtext is not advice. It's a value judgment.

Unlike with themes or morals, you never state the Subtext. If you do, your humor writing will fall apart. It's called Subtext because it's concealed under the text and never revealed except inside the reader's mind.

It's like a subway. It travels underground. If it traveled at street level, pedestrians, cars, and everything else would get plowed over as it crashed through everything in sight. This havoc is a fitting analogy for what happens to your humor writing when you state your Subtext.

SCIENCE FICTION

Science Fiction, a genre of storytelling that emerged in the 19th century, has a lot in common with Satire. By looking closely at science fiction, we can better understand Subtext and how it works in Satire.

Many of the same techniques for writing humor discussed in this book are employed in the best science-fiction stories. Foremost among these techniques is the use of Subtext. Science fiction is essentially Satire but instead of using humor to communicate Subtext, it uses the awe of science, the future, aliens, or worlds yet unknown.

Virtually all science-fiction stories have a sobering, progressive message beneath the surface text of the story. For example, H. G. Wells' War of the Worlds, one of the earliest and greatest science-fiction novels, says, "Humanity's arrogance as the dominant species may be unwarranted." George Orwell's 1984 says, "Totalitarianism destroys souls."

Science-fiction Subtext is easy to spot. It's typically a problem in our time and place played out in another time and place. In Satire, Subtext is more hidden, but it serves the same purpose.

In Satire, the Subtext is revealed in each joke. In a longer form of writing, each joke (or "joke beat") is spaced out in the writing so the writer can exercise some control over when the reader laughs, and when the reader gets a break from laughing, creating just the right pace.

To some degree, Subtext is subjective. What one person reads into a piece of humor writing may be different from another person. The skilled comedy writer aims to make the Subtext of any joke as clear as possible, to control the message being delivered to the reader.

You don't want to leave humor writing too open to interpretation. You don't want to shoot your message with a shotgun, spraying out ideas that lead to a variety of broad interpretations—this is the realm of fine art and other non-comedic modes of expression. In comedy, you want to shoot with a laser rifle, to avoid any possible misinterpretation of your message. If people misinterpret your message, they may not get your joke.

Subtext is the most important part of your writing. Jokes by themselves without much Subtext are a fun yet somewhat empty experience. As a writer, you have one mission: to communicate ideas to readers. Your Subtext is where those ideas are. They're not in your literal text. Your literal text is merely the delivery medium—a UPS truck. What you want your readers to get is the precious cargo inside—the stuff they ordered. Those are the core ideas you want to communicate.

It can be awkward to try to articulate Subtext because we normally don't say it out loud—we only think it. But to write successful humor, you need to be aware of your Subtext.

You also need to be in total control of it. You need to know what Subtext you intend to communicate, and you need to orchestrate its optimal discovery by the reader. That's the singular skill of the humor writer.

By the same token, comedy is not math. You need to allow for a little wiggle room in the articulating of Subtext. You will naturally get different opinions from different readers as to what exactly the Subtext of a given work of Satire is trying to communicate. Nonetheless, the goal of the writer must always be as little variance in interpretation as possible.

Subtext can usually be stated in a simple sentence: subject, verb, object. And it must be irreducible. It can have no hidden meaning in itself. If your Subtext has a hidden meaning, or deeper Subtext, or is itself trying to be funny or tell a joke, then it's not your true Subtext. The Subtext of any piece of humor writing is a simple statement of opinion. Furthermore, it must be coherent, something people will understand.

You can identify Subtext by looking closely at a single funny line and asking yourself, "what is this line really saying?" What you'll find is that once the joke is deconstructed, it's communicating a strong value judgment or opinion held by the writer, an observation about life.

Former *Colbert Report* writer Dan Guterman is one of the best joke writers in the world. He issues a steady stream of great jokes on his Twitter feed (@danguterman). Here are some, broken down into their subtextual message:

> *Don't forget: Tomorrow is Bring Your*
> *Daughter To Tears Day.*

Subtext: The idea of Take Your Daughter to Work Day is sad, that in our society girls (not boys) need this extra exposure to the workplace.

> *Couldn't get tickets to the Daytona 500,*
> *so I just stayed home and set a box of*
> *Tide on fire.*

Subtext: NASCAR is a pathetic, too-heavily sponsored sport, and it's a twisted fact that many people watch if for the accidents.

> *Fun Fact: If you stretched out your intes-*
> *tines they would reach all the way to the*
> *cabin in the woods you were murdered in.*

Subtext: It's a little unsettling when people point out how long our intestines are.

Notice how in each of these jokes, the Subtext points out a problem with humanity or society. The best satirical Subtext does this. That is, in fact, the role of Satire.

Guterman uses so many Funny Filters (chapter 6) as well as techniques to create edginess (page 78) that it's often difficult to define his Subtext narrowly—there's a lot going on in each joke, and they can be interpreted in slightly different ways. Subtext is somewhat subjective, but his jokes aim well, so there's not a lot of room for misinterpretation, and wherever you come out, you're tapping a rich vein of Guterman's opinion on any given subject.

> FUNNY-WRITING TIP #9: KNOW WHAT JOKE YOU'RE TELLING, AND BE SURE YOUR READER KNOWS WHAT JOKE YOU'RE TELLING
>
> *Always be in control of your message by using clear, intentional Subtext. Never leave a joke open to interpretation. When you ask yourself, "What is my joke really saying?" you need to have a specific answer. You need to know what your Subtext is, and how you're revealing it to your readers. If you don't know what you're saying, or why you think it should be funny, you have no control over what Subtext your readers might discover, no control over how they discover it, and therefore almost no chance they'll laugh at it.*

Humor writing Subtext does not need to be funny. In fact, it usually isn't. "People are cruel," is a subtextual message that's been used to great effect by many Satirists. "Racism is wrong," worked well for Mark Twain. "Totalitarian government is dehumanizing" and "Power corrupts" worked very well for George Orwell. Subtext that's worked well for other satirists over the years: "Relationships are not special"; "People who have kids are selfish"; "Governments are incompetent"; "We're all slaves."

Not only are some of these not funny—many are downright sad, even scary! This kind of dark Subtext can make for extremely powerful and memorable humor writing. Steve Allen said, "Comedy equals tragedy plus time." In fact, he believed the source of all comedy was tragedy.

Todd Hanson, *The Onion*'s head writer for many years and one of the handful of people instrumental in forging *The Onion*'s uniquely dark and sardonic style, said humor is about one thing: "life's nightmare hellscape of unrelenting horror."

Don't discount the power of tragedy, either in your own life or in the collective life of humanity, to make for powerful Subtext that can lead to some of the most richly satisfying humor.

HOW TO WRITE SUBTEXT

Do you have any opinions? Do you feel passionately about anything? Do you have ideas about life, people, the world, and what's wrong with everything? Of course you do. We all do. And that's all you need to make great Subtext.

There are two simple methods you can use to create Subtext.

First, look through your notebook of ideas or a Morning Pages exercise you've written. These are glimpses into what madness is floating around in your subconscious mind—disconnected opinions, thoughts or ideas yearning for some kind of expression. These are notions bubbling up from the darkest caverns of your intellect that on some level you care about. Maybe you didn't realize you cared about them until they popped out of you in one of these exercises. But they popped out all the same, and now you can use them. Some of these opinions or observations could be Subtext in themselves, some might reveal a deeper Subtext. Either way, try to dig down to the core message.

> FUNNY-WRITING TIP #10: COMFORT THE AFFLICTED, AFFLICT THE COMFORTABLE
>
> *This tip comes from journalism, but it works for Satire, too. If the target of your Satire is the downtrodden, such as the homeless, or victims of a tragedy, it will come across as mean-spirited, and audiences won't find it funny. You can make a joke about anything you want, but the target must deserve ridicule. The best targets are usually "the comfortable": the status quo, an entrenched power, or any authority, no matter how low-level.*

Second, generate some jokes or ideas that you think are funny using the Morning Pages' just-move-your-fingers-and-keep-writing approach. Then later, when you have your Editor hat on, read through those ideas and ask yourself what the resulting misshapen half-jokes are really saying—what's the Subtext? If you detect an interesting and unique opinion or value judgment, there's a good possibility you have a joke that could work, and you should consider refining it.

In the next chapter, you'll find specific tools for refining a joke, and transforming Subtext, which is often not very funny by itself, into jokes that are actually funny.

CHAPTER 5 ACTION STEPS

1. Look at your exercise from the last chapter, your 10 jokes, and determine what the Subtext is for each joke. What is your joke really saying when you strip away the humor? Try to write out the Subtext of each joke using a simple subject-verb-object sentence.

2. Write 10 different Subtext ideas. These shouldn't necessarily be funny; they're just opinions or value judgments like, "We're destroying our planet," "People without a legitimate handicap shouldn't be allowed to ride mobility scooters in the grocery store," or "Dogs are dumb."

6

THE 11 FUNNY FILTERS

The Subtext of any joke must be thinly veiled, and there are 11 different ways to veil it. By filtering your Subtext though one of these 11 Funny Filters, you create a barrier between your reader and you—more specifically, between your reader and your intended Subtext—allowing the reader to add two and two to discover your hidden message.

That discovery results in a laugh. This is how all jokes work.

They're called Funny Filters because the humor writer starts with Subtext, which is not usually very humorous, then filters it through one or more Funny Filters so it comes out the other end as a joke.

There may be other ways to make people laugh besides these 11 Funny Filters. Just about anything can make someone laugh at the right time, under the right circumstances, and in the right context. However, if something causes someone to laugh that's not one of the 11 Funny Filters, that's not a reliable or repeatable occurrence. What the 11 Funny Filters offer is a level of objectivity and predictability.

To appeal to the widest possible audience, the humor writer must create a situation in which jokes have the best chance to succeed. In professional comedy writing, only these 11 Funny Filters will meet with consistent success. If a piece of your writing doesn't employ at least one of the 11 Funny Filters, or it's not using the Funny Filter(s) properly, very few in your audience will find it funny. If you use the Funny Filters as directed, most in your audience will find your writing funny most of the time.

And that, as we've established, is the most objectivity and predictability you get in comedy: the chance for a good batting average.

Each Funny Filter is described here in no particular order.

FUNNY FILTER 1: IRONY

Irony happens when the literal meaning of what you write is the opposite of the intended meaning. "Opposite" is the key word. Irony is all about opposites. If the Subtext you want to communicate is "nuns are weird," you would use Irony to create a joke by expressing the opposite opinion: "Nuns are perfectly sane," or "There's nothing strange about dressing in a cumbersome headdress, locking yourself in a church and avoiding sex for the rest of your life."

The trick to Irony is heightening the contrast so that the two things you're contrasting are truly polar opposites.

When you learn to drive, the instructor may have referred to the proper steering-wheel hand position as "9 and 3"—hands on opposite ends of the wheel, giving you maximum leverage to turn in either direction. "10 and 2" would be hands too close together, giving you less leverage to control the vehicle in an emergency. Think of contrast in Irony in the same way.

You're playing a fun game with your readers—they want to see how far you'll go to espouse the opposite of your opinion.

Here are some headlines from *The Onion* that use Irony:

• *Alcoholic Father Disappointed In Pothead Son*

• *Cool 'Cybergranny' Needs Machines To Help Her Live*
• *Mother Theresa Sent To Hell In Wacky Afterlife Mix-Up*
• *It's Not A Crack House, It's A Crack Home*

FUNNY-WRITING TIP #11: HEIGHTEN CONTRAST

Humor often involves the contrasting of two things, whether it's the straight character and jokester, two opposing ends of an ironic situation, or a fake world and the real world. A common flaw in a lot of unsuccessful humor is that the contrast inherent in the joke is not heightened enough. By simply heightening the contrast to its greatest possible extreme, a lot of comedy writing is made instantly funnier.

Irony can sometimes be confused with the "Ol' Switcheroo," which is when a joke turns out differently than expected. Turning out differently is not the same as turning out the opposite, which is the key to Irony. Switcheroos also happen when two things trade places in a joke. "Man Bites Dog" is a well-worn example.

The Ol' Switcheroo is sometimes used to construct remedial jokes, often in comic strips and mediocre sitcoms. ("Did you take the dog out?" "I couldn't." "Why not?" "The dog took *me* out!")

Irony is also sometimes confused with Sarcasm. Sarcasm is "Irony light"—a watered-down version that's delivered with an annoyed attitude that exposes its Subtext in an all-too-knowing way. For example, a teenager might try to get a laugh by saying, "I'm *so* excited to get up and go to school today."

Sarcasm isn't all that funny because it's not believable. Sarcasm isn't trying very hard to fool anyone.

By contrast, when you use Irony as a literary device in Satire, you pretend to adopt the opposite of your true message with absolute conviction, and you play it straight.

Neither Switcheroos nor Sarcasm count as Funny Filters, and can't be trusted to make professional-quality jokes.

IRONY SUMMARY:
WHAT IT IS: Extreme Opposites
HOW TO USE IT: Write the polar opposite of your Subtext.

FUNNY FILTER 2: CHARACTER

Character is the most popular Funny Filter. It's used almost exclusively on every comedy TV show, comedy movie, and most sketch and improv shows. It's the great engine behind virtually all performance-based comedy. Character is important in prose as well, but, like all the Funny Filters, it works especially well—and makes for more layered, literary humor—when used in combination with other Funny Filters.

The idea behind Character is simple: When a comedic character acts on his, her or its clearly defined traits, a joke results.

The key is that the character must be comedic. A comedic character is a simply drawn, two-dimensional character who has no more than 1–3 traits, which the reader is made aware of through the character's actions or simple exposition.

Comedic characters aren't meant to be realistic like dramatic characters. Dramatic characters are meant to seem three-dimensional, like flesh-and-blood people with nuance, contradictions and complex histories. Readers want to feel like they actually know dramatic characters. Writers often write long bios for these characters, figuring out what they eat for breakfast, where they went to elementary school, who their ancestors were, and so on.

Comedic characters are much simpler. You don't want to write a long, detailed bio for a comedic character. You just want to list 1–3 traits. Comedic characters aren't meant to seem real. They're merely meant to represent a fundamental flaw that all human beings share. We can all relate to a comedic character who symbolizes one of our core weaknesses. Laughing at them allows us to laugh at ourselves and the inherent foibles that make us all alike. Readers don't see comedic characters as real, and they don't want to. They expect them to be little more than symbols.

That's not to say that a comedic character can't be effective in dramatic writing. The Character Funny Filter can be applied to any kind of writing, dramatic included. Any time a dramatic piece of writing needs a joke or a funny moment, it relies on one of the 11 Funny Filters, most commonly Character.

It may be a jarring shift in tone to introduce a comedic character with less than three traits into a serious story with, say, a well-rounded main character who's a cancer survivor. So, the tonal treatment of each character must be managed carefully. A character who's friends with this main character, who has maybe one dominant character trait but is otherwise realistic, could serve as an excellent source of comic relief in a story like that.

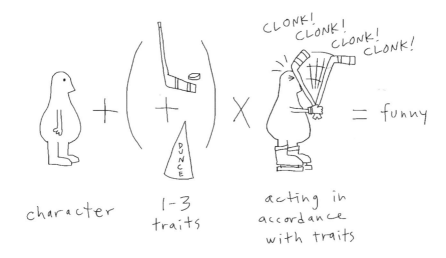

character   1-3 traits   acting in accordance with traits

Even a dramatic lead character can be made comedic during a short sequence or scene—as long as one or two traits of the character that are more comedic than dramatic (simple traits that reveal a relatable flaw) are brought to the fore during that scene, and the character acts on those simple traits. This can serve to create a funny moment in an otherwise serious, dramatic story. For example, when JoBeth Williams encounters the Kramers' son in the middle of the night in *Kramer vs. Kramer*. It's a dramatic movie with dramatic characters, but this scene is made funny by reducing Williams' character to 1–3 traits: she's naked and embarrassed. Other Funny Filters, including Irony and Shock (Funny Filter 3), are also employed, making the scene a near-guaranteed laugh.

> FUNNY-WRITING TIP #12: USE VERISIMILITUDE
> *If you're copying something else in form, which you'll often do in Satire (be it a pattern of speech, a character, or another work of entertainment), you must make it as similar to the thing you're imitating as possible. If it's a senator character, for example, he should talk like real senators talk. If it's a Parody of, say, an advertisement, it should sound as much like a real advertisement as possible. Be consistent, play it straight, and never "break voice."*

Most stand-up comedians use the Character Funny Filter to create a character for themselves, their "persona." These are case studies in the Character Funny Filter and how simple it is to use: Bill Burr is the psycho who ironically makes sense; Marc Maron is the anxiety-ridden over-sharer; David Spade is the Know-It-All. All comedians have these 1–3 unique traits and often open their acts by defining their traits so they can get laughs acting accordingly. Other comedians skip the exposition and just start telling jokes in which they act on their traits.

ARCHETYPES

There are several classic Character Archetypes, characters who have been used and reused in prose and performance comedy for centuries. Many of them come from the Italian Renaissance theater (the *Commedia Dell'Arte*), but some have their origins even earlier, in ancient Greek theater. Certain characters keep coming back because they have universally appealing qualities, and audiences love them. They include the Dummy, the Slob, the Snob, the Know-It-All, the Everyperson, the Grown-up Child, the Klutz, the Lothario, the Nerd, the Robot (or straight person), the Naif, the Bumbling Authority, and the Trickster. There are many others.

Most of these characters are self-explanatory. The Grown-up Child is a character who acts with far more emotion than situations require, often bawling and throwing tantrums like a child. This character represents the child in all of us. Will Ferrell almost always plays the Grown-up Child, as did Lucille Ball. As didThe Robot is a character who acts with far less emotion that situations require. This is the "straight man" of comedy.

The Bumbling Authority is the blowhard in charge, usually flashing some kind of badge or official emblem indicating station or rank. The Bumbling Authority talks big, but is an obvious fool. This Archetype represents our leaders' incompetence. People have always mistrusted their "betters," and few things entertain audiences more than seeing authorities or elites brought down to size. This defining trait is precisely what makes the Bumbling Authority Archetype so popular.

> ### STEREOTYPES
> *Archetypes are not stereotypes. Stereotypes are Archetypes gone wrong, when a foreign people or, worse, an oppressed minority population, are characterized with derogatory traits. Archetypes, on the other hand, are universal, and aren't specific to any race or nationality. Stereotypes, like clichés, should never be used in comedy. They're a red flag to readers, signifying bad writing. The only justifiable reason to use stereotypes in comedy is when you're making fun of them, or the people who use them, or otherwise deconstructing or commenting on them in an enlightened way.*

Ralph Kramden on *The Honeymooners* is one example of a Bumbling Authority. Lt. Frank Drebin from *Police Squad* is another. A few more: *Ace Ventura: Pet Detective;* Ron Burgundy from the *Anchorman* movies *(who, because he's played by Will Ferrell, is also a Grown-up Child). The Onion* is a Bumbling Authority character. It purports to be a serious and official engine of truth in the world, yet it spouts nonsense.

One fascinating character often used as the driving force in comedy is the Trickster. The Trickster plays games and can violate the rules of society or even reality in order to win. The Trickster has its origins in African mythology where it's often a rabbit or fox. Dr. Seuss was a master of the Trickster, using him for *Cat in the Hat, Fox in Socks* and other classic books. In movies, Ferris Bueller is a well-known Trickster. Bill Murray, in his heyday in the 1980s, often played Tricksters.

For a comprehensive example of classic modern character Archetypes, you needn't look further than *Looney Tunes*. In many ways this is the *Commedia Dell'Arte* for the modern age. Bugs Bunny is a classic Trickster. Daffy Duck is a Bumbling Authority (often assaying roles as sheriffs, commanders or other low-level authorities) who always proves himself a fool. Elmer Fudd is the Dummy. Pepé LePew is the Lothario.

When selecting a main character, it's often a good idea to use an Archetype. Archetypes are a proven success that have been beloved for eons. Secondary and tertiary characters are less critical, and can get by as quirky, non-Archetypes. In any case, we needn't limit ourselves to stock characters in prose. And we may not want to. Archetypes can have a tendency to come off as clichés because they've been used so often, especially if no effort is made to distinguish them from similar Archetypes of the past. Comedy always works better when characters sparkle with originality.

To create original comedic characters, you can use one of two methods:

One, you can think up someone with a nice mix of 1–3 traits. A nice mix of traits in comedy often involves some Irony. For example, an insurance actuary who wishes he were a football player, yet is a weakling constantly stricken with illness. This method of character creation is perfectly acceptable. However, unless your character fits an established Archetype, it may not resonate with audiences.

Two, you can use one of the Archetypes, but reinvent it. You can make Archetypes feel fresh by doing one of three things: (1) give them a job or station that we've never seen before, (Example: Ace Ventura is the Bumbling Authority, but he's a pet detective); (2) make them a race, creed, species or thing we've never seen before (Example: Mr. Peabody is the Know-It-All, but he's a dog); or (3) put them in an environment we've never seen them in before (Example: in *The Hitchhikers Guide to the Galaxy*, Arthur Dent is the Everyperson, but he's in outer space, thus becoming another popular Archetype, the Fish out of Water).

Some one-liner examples of the Character Funny Filter:

> *I don't get no respect at all. The other*
> *night I felt like having a drink. I said to*
> *the bartender, 'Surprise me.' He showed*
> *me a naked picture of my wife.*
> —RODNEY DANGERFIELD

Note how Dangerfield establishes his one trait (that he gets no respect), then presents an example of his acting in accordance with that one trait (or in his case, his being acted upon in accordance with the trait, which is another way to reveal the trait).

> *Philandering String Theorist Can*
> *Explain Everything*
> —THE ONION

This a textbook Character joke. It establishes two traits: (1) he's a philanderer and (2) he's a string theorist. Then it shows him acting on both those traits at the same time in a double entendre (a product of Wordplay, Funny Filter 5).

CHARACTER SUMMARY:

WHAT IT IS: A comedic character or character Archetype with 1–3 clear traits.

HOW TO USE IT: Show the character act in accordance with their traits.

For more on Character, check out my book How to Write Funny Characters.

FUNNY FILTER 3: SHOCK

Sex, swearing, violence, or any overt gross-out are the go-to tools of Shock. This Funny Filter encompasses anything that would be inappropriate to mention in mixed company.

Shock startles readers into laughter, and shakes them out of the polite, civilized box society tends to squeeze us into without our realizing it. And it works wonders. It loosens people up and gets them laughing.

Shock can range from mild to extreme. A joke can have just a dash of Shock, or it can have an overdose, depending on what's required to communicate the Subtext.

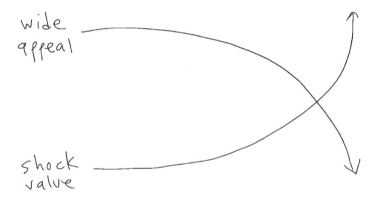

In most instances, Shock is best used as a garnish, not the main course. As a main course, its audience is limited. Just about everyone enjoys a little Shock in their humor. Humor, after all, comes from surprise, and shock is simply an amped-up kind of surprise. Fourteen-year-old boys (and those with a 14-year-old boy sensibility) like it best of all. In fact, they can't get enough of it. You can target that demographic quite easily by overloading your work with Shock. But beware—the more Shock you use, and the weaker your Subtext, the more you alienate the rest of the audience. Fourteen-year-old boys don't require any Subtext in their Shock humor.

And that's the most important guideline to remember about Shock: a little goes a long way. Individual writers have to be the judge of how much is too much for their audience. A good rule of thumb is, if you think it's gratuitous, it probably is.

Shock is best used in service of good Subtext. When used in moderation and with good Subtext, Shock can appeal to not just the 14-year-old boys, but everyone else, too. A good example of shock humor done well is the spread in *America: The Book* that shows the nine Supreme Court justices naked. Seeing old, out-of-shape people naked is inherently funny for its Shock value, but this stunt had good Subtext as well: Supreme Court justices, and therefore the laws they uphold, are not infallible; they're (visibly) flawed just like the rest of us.

POOPING AND FARTING

Amateur humor writers often turn to pooping and farting with the expectation that instant and hardy laughs will result. They consider these and other bodily functions a trump card. And we can hardly blame them. Gross-out or shocking references like these technically qualify as legitimate, professional humor when used properly (that is, in moderation and/or in service of good Subtext). The problem with most amateur pooping and farting humor is that it's not used in moderation, and it rarely has any Subtext.

The human butt is the single funniest thing in the known universe. This is undisputed. Any time a human butt is referenced, seen, or used in a joke, the effect is immediate: everybody laughs. But it's important to recognize that the butt is a one-trick pony. It can serve as a great addition to an already clever joke or humor sequence (i.e., one that uses multiple Funny Filters and good Subtext), but by itself, it quickly wears out its welcome.

Amateur humor writers don't realize this fact, so they often milk the butt for as many poop and fart jokes as they can. They also don't realize that it's the butt that's the funniest thing in the universe, not the pooping and farting.

Pooping is a serious gross-out reference. Those 14-year-old boys will laugh at your poop jokes, but you'll lose everyone else almost immediately.

Fart jokes are of a slightly different order. They are, in fact, the H-bomb of comedy. We all recognize the power of farts to generate near-universal laughs, and it's easy to imagine winning the war of comedy instantly and decisively by just "dropping the fart bomb on 'em." But it's worth considering what happens after an H-bomb is detonated: everything is destroyed. You can use fart jokes to get your big laughs, but once you've used the most powerful weapon in the humor arsenal, how are you going to follow it up?

Because they're so lowbrow, a lot of humor writers avoid fart jokes altogether. They consider them too easy, the domain of amateurs.

When professional comedy writers brave the subject of the fart, they abide by an unspoken tradition to try to make the funniest fart joke possible. Just making fart noises to get a laugh is considered crass, so if they're harnessing the immense power of the fart, they must do it masterfully, so as not to come off as taking advantage of the "easy out."

Some of the best examples of great fart jokes are Steve Martin's "farting section on airplanes" bit, *Blazing Saddles'* campfire scene, and *Mr. Show's* "dueling fartists."

EDGY COMEDY

Comedy that's "edgy" is in great demand in the entertainment business. A lot of comedy writers mistakenly believe that by simply increasing the Shock value of humor, edgy comedy will result. This is not the case, as the unfortunate *Movie 43* demonstrated. The movie was promoted as a dangerously edgy comedy, but contained nothing more than Shock humor with no Subtext and certainly no moderation.

Quality edgy humor is achieved in one of three ways:

1. Using the Shock Funny Filter in moderation and with astute Subtext.

2. Decreasing the amount of time in the equation "comedy equals tragedy plus time."

3. Appearing to violate the first half of Funny-Writing Tip #10 ("Comfort the Afflicted, Afflict the Comfortable," page 64). By appearing to go after the wrong target (the afflicted), or getting tantalizingly close to hitting it, all while being very careful to hit the right target (the comfortable), you will create edgy comedy. This is a tricky move, because if you don't manage this illusion skillfully, and instead are perceived by audiences as hitting the wrong target, your humor will not only be unfunny, it will be reviled.

formula for edgy comedy:

comedy = tragedy

Here are a couple of one-liners that use Shock:

> *You can't fight City Hall, but you can*
> *goddamn sure blow it up.*
> —GEORGE CARLIN

Carlin uses swearing and violence in this simple one-liner. This is Shock in moderation revealing a very interesting Subtext: We all feel powerless and enraged when it comes to the incompetence of government, and it's even possible to understand the rage of a terrorist, because we've all felt it to some degree. Even Carlin's Subtext is shocking!

> *When God gives you AIDS, make*
> *lemonaids.*
>
> —SARAH SILVERMAN

Using a shocking AIDS reference (and several other Funny Filters), Silverman reveals her Subtext: the positive-thinking pablum we say to ourselves is woefully inadequate in the face of the true darkness of life.

I like to think of Shock as a dash of cayenne pepper in humor. It's usually best when there's only a hint of it. It takes an experienced chef to know the right amount, but with practice, you'll find it. And when you do, you'll be creating some deliciously spicy comedy.

SHOCK SUMMARY:
WHAT IT IS: Anything shocking (sex, violence, swearing, or a gross-out).
HOW TO USE IT: In moderation, and always with Subtext. The more
shocking the humor, the more astute the Subtext needs to be.

FUNNY FILTER 4: HYPERBOLE

Hyperbole is another word for exaggeration. Hyperbole the Funny Filter, however, is "exaggeration plus." When using Hyperbole to generate laughs, the writer needs to exaggerate not just a little, and even a lot may not do the trick. To make readers laugh with Hyperbole, the writer needs to exaggerate so greatly that the laws of science or reason are violated.

This type of comedic Hyperbole is the source of a lot of classic one-liners, the kinds of jokes Borscht Belt comedians used to tell. Rodney Dangerfield is a good example. So many of his one-liners used Hyperbole and Character. He was the guy who didn't get any respect, so one of his jokes was, "My parents didn't like me. For bathtub toys they gave me a blender and a transistor radio." Obviously, if he had played with those things in the bathtub, he'd be dead, which defies both science and reason. This joke has a dash of Shock as well since it suggests the violent death of a child.

Hyperbole allows you to get to ridiculous extremes by exaggerating so far beyond reality that you're suddenly in a different, impossible reality. Joan Rivers was always fond of calling out Hollywood starlets for being overweight. One of her one-liners could be repurposed to apply to any target she wanted: "She's so fat she's my two best friends." It's the sheer impossibility of this Hyperbole that made it work every time she used it. It's a textbook example of a classic Borscht Belt-style Hyperbole. By now, though, it's an old joke, so it counts as a cliché. The Rodney Dangerfield joke exaggerates how little respect he got. The Joan Rivers joke exaggerates how fat her target was. They both do it to an absurd, impossible extreme.

Most writers instinctively think of Hyperbole as a literary device that exaggerates what's big or what's negative. It's worth noting that Hyperbole doesn't always have to go that way. You can exaggerate small or positive, or any direction. It depends what you're trying to say with your Subtext. But in all cases, the way you use Hyperbole is to start with your Subtext, then exaggerate it one way or other, and see if anything funny comes of it.

Hyperbole, more than any other Funny Filter, feels like real joke-writing. When you hyperbolize well, you'll feel like you're writing professional jokes, because this is one tool professionals use a lot.

Some other one-liners using Hyperbole:

> *I gave my doctor a urine sample. It had*
> *an olive in it.*
> —RODNEY DANGERFIELD

> *NRA Calls For Teachers to Keep Loaded*
> *Gun Pointed At Class for Entire School*
> *Day*
> —THE ONION

It's so cold here in Washington, D.C., the politicians have their hands in their own pockets.

—Bob Hope

You can see how simple Hyperbole is: just exaggerated Subtext and make a point with gusto. But while it may be simple to recognize and describe, Hyperbole is challenging to write.

The Subtext of the Rodney Dangerfield sample is "I drink too much." The Subtext of *The Onion*'s is that the NRA has an extreme view on gun rights.

The Subtext of the Bob Hope joke is that politicians are money-grubbers. But like many of Bob Hope's jokes, it's quite sophisticated and has a lot of other things going on. (This high quality is the result of the dozens of joke writers Hope employed. Quantity, as we know, is the key to quality.) He's not just using Hyperbole in this joke. He's also using Character, two layers of Irony, a second layer of Hyperbole, and a few other Funny Filters as well (we'll cover them all in this chapter). The Character is the politicians, who have one trait: they always have their hands in other people's pockets. The Irony is how the politicians are acting: they're acting in the opposite way from what you'd expect. (This is called Character Irony, a standard pairing of these two Funny Filters.) The second layer of Hyperbole is Metahumor (Funny Filter 11). He's using the clichéd "It's so cold here..." joke introduction, a standard set-up normally associated with a Hyperbole joke, but his Hyperbole is not impossible or beyond reason at all (politicians having their hands in someone else's pockets is quite easy, physically). However, doing it in an ironic context makes its inherent non-impossibleness seem impossible, and therefore Hyperbolic.

Note also how short all of these one-liners are. There's not an unnecessary word among them.

HYPERBOLE SUMMARY:
WHAT IT IS: Exaggeration so absurd it goes beyond the bounds of science or reason.

HOW TO USE IT: Exaggerate your Subtext.

FUNNY FILTER 5: WORDPLAY

Wordplay is any kind of fun you can have with words.

Broadly speaking, the Wordplay Funny Filter covers any use of words beyond their standard meaning(s) or beyond their inherent function as words.

Specifically, Wordplay can take any number of forms: revealing double or triple meanings (entendre); making up new words; puns; word switches; the repetition of words; playing with the sounds of words. The list of named Wordplay devices is too long to recite here, but here's a short sampling of some that can make for excellent humor:

- *Anagrams*
- *Spoonerisms*
- *Oxymorons*
- *Tongue Twisters*
- *Rhymes (best used in song or poetry*
  written in verse, not in prose)
- *Rebuses*
- *Puns*

Another game of Wordplay you can play is using words that sound funny. *Balloon, Thwack, Feeble, Clump*, and other words that are simply fun to say or sound funny, can add an excellent note of humor to just about any joke. This technique is closely related to Funny Filter 7.

Oxymorons can be somewhat amusing if original, but be careful. "It's an oxymoron, like Military Intelligence," is a cliché that's been around for many years.

The comic strip "Family Circus" nearly pushed the Wordplay device known as Malapropism out of fashion, turning the device, for a couple of generations, into a roundly ridiculed cliché used solely to reference the cute verbal slip-ups of toddlers, like "Pasghetti" for "Spaghetti." Malapropisms enjoyed a resurgence in the 2000s with Bushisms, which were funnier because they also employed a layer of the Character and Irony Funny Filters. (The Character: George W. Bush as the Dummy Archetype. The Irony: the Dummy is the polar opposite type of character you would want or expect in a President of the United States.)

FUNNY-WRITING TIP #13: PLAY IT STRAIGHT

Mark Twain said it best: "The humorous story is told gravely; the teller does his best to conceal the fact that he even dimly suspects that there is anything funny about it." Don't wink at the audience. Don't be cute. Don't laugh along with your jokes. When you appear convincingly unaware that you're trying to be amusing, when you use verisimilitude to remain true to a "straight person" voice—regardless how ridiculous and humorous the ideas you're presenting—this is what we call "playing it straight." The contrast you create between your sober delivery and your hilarious material adds an important layer of Irony to your humor. The way Leslie Nielsen played Lt. Frank Drebin in Police Squad *and the* Naked Gun *Movies is a defining example of how to play it straight. The Onion's strict AP style is another.*

Some established Wordplay varieties aren't funny. This could be because they've been used too much and come off as clichés, or maybe, for whatever reason, they're out of fashion at the moment. They can also seem clever for cleverness's sake, and very difficult to use in service of great Subtext.

These types of Wordplay are best avoided in satirical writing:

- *Alliteration*
- *Acronyms*
- *Pangrams*

- *Mnemonics*
- *Tom Swifties and Wellerisms*
- *Typewriter Words*
- *Subalphabetic Words*

However, there is a way to make use of all types of Wordplay, including the "best avoided" list above, and that's by making fun of them, or deconstructing them, which we'll explore in greater depth in Funny Filter 11.

In prose writing, Wordplay is especially useful in titles, headlines and

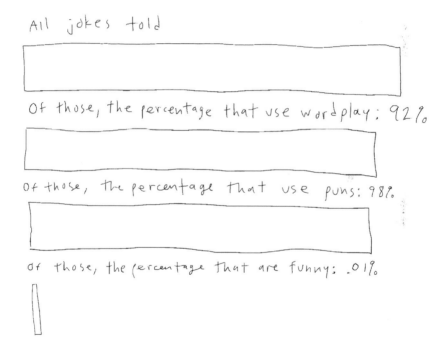

All jokes told

Of those, the percentage that use wordplay: 92%

Of those, the percentage that use puns: 98%

Of those, the percentage that are funny: .01%

specific jokes as opposed to informing a larger structure like Irony and Character can.

Most jokes in circulation at any given time employ Wordplay, but these jokes aren't usually very funny because their Wordplay isn't crafted well. The simplistic pun-based jokes that tend to go around aren't going to dazzle anyone. These not-so-great jokes ("groaners") are primarily puns with no Subtext, like, "How did the frog die? He croaked." This type of

Wordplay involving one word that has two meanings offers no additional Subtext beyond "this word has two meanings," which is not very astute and certainly doesn't point out any great wrong in the world.

This is the level of sophistication we typically see in children's joke books and on Laffy Taffy packages.

Bad or simple Wordplay often only makes sense one way and not the other. In the frog example above, the joke only makes sense if you take the meaning of the word "croaked" to be "died." It doesn't make any sense if you take the meaning as "talked like a frog." One simple step to improving puns is to at least make sure all meanings of the words you use make sense no matter which way you read the joke. Example: "What did the frog say to the newspaper coupon? Rip-it." This joke is slightly less of a groaner because it at least makes sense both ways.

Layering different Wordplay devices is a good way to achieve more sophistication in Wordplay, and that usually means experimenting with more than just one simple pun. However, there can be diminishing returns with this tactic and you risk over-complicating the joke. (See Funny-Writing Tip #18, "Keep It Simple," page 119.)

The Onion's excellent story, "Fritolaysia Cuts Off Chiplomatic Relations With Snakistan," written by Mike DiCenzo, makes use of so much simple, single-minded wordplay that its overwhelming effect is part of the joke:

> *KARUNCHI, SNAKISTAN—Citing crumbling relations due to years of protracted french-onion diplomacy, the president of the Central Asian doritocracy Fritolaysia withdrew the country's ambassadors from Snakistan Monday . . .*

The story is also rich with Subtext: Americans don't care about turmoil in countries halfway around the world; they care about snacks—two veins of Subtext often tapped by *The Onion*.

The most important rule of thumb with Wordplay, and a great way to give it the sophistication it needs, is to always make sure you're working with good Subtext. The difference between a groaner and a sophisticated, genuinely funny Wordplay joke is often as simple as that: a groaner is Wordplay without Subtext, a successful joke is Wordplay with Subtext, especially astute Subtext.

Another important guideline to keep in mind when using Wordplay is Funny-Writing Tip #13 ("Play It Straight," page 84). More than any other Funny Filter, Wordplay risks exposing the writer's effort to be overly clever or cute, which readers will perceive as a wink. This effort becomes far more obvious when there's poor Subtext or none at all.

Like Shock, good Wordplay is often no more than a garnish on humor writing. As the main thrust of the writing (again, unless used in service of good Subtext), Wordplay can feel too lightweight to generate sizable laughs.

Some examples of Wordplay used in one-liners:

> *I put a dollar in a change machine.*
> *Nothing changed.*
>
> —GEORGE CARLIN

> *I spilled spot remover on my dog. Now*
> *he's gone.*
>
> —STEVEN WRIGHT

> *Echolocation, Echolocation,*
> *Echolocation—the 3 most important*
> *things in bat real estate.*
>
> —ME

Note that each of these jokes has Subtext. The Subtext of the first is that societal change is difficult. The second, Spot is an odd name for a dog, since it's the same as a stain. (There's also Shock in this one, since the dog disappeared, presumably destroyed by the spot remover.) The third, that old joke about "the three most important things in real estate" is a dumb cliché.

WORDPLAY SUMMARY:
WHAT IT IS: Playing with words in ways beyond their standard definitions.
HOW TO USE IT: Only with good Subtext.

FUNNY FILTER 6: REFERENCE

Reference is perhaps the most useful of all the Funny Filters, even more so than the ubiquitous Character. Reference is at the core of almost all humor. Most of the other Funny Filters, for example, employ a Reference at some level, and most Subtext is based on Reference.

A Reference is a relatable observation. Readers have seen, heard or otherwise experienced the thing being referenced. It makes them say, "Oh, yeah, I've experienced that—and I didn't know others had!" This reaction makes them laugh.

The more unique and relevant the Reference, the more sophisticated it will be perceived to be, and the more the audience will enjoy it. The less unique or relevant the Reference, the closer you get to cliché territory.

Reference is closely related to Observational Humor, which is the observing and pointing out of the little things in everyday life that you have in common with your audience, especially things that they haven't consciously thought about before.

But the Reference Funny Filter is broader than everyday observations. It's a reference to any shared experience that the writer and audience have in common. And that's what tickles the funny bone with Reference—it bonds writer and reader, or performer and audience. When their shared experience is revealed, especially one that audiences feel like they're hearing for the first time, the audience connects with the comedy writer on a deeper level. They feel like the writer has a secret insight into their everyday life, which they find delightful.

Jerry Seinfeld is probably the best-known master of Reference humor. "Did you ever notice how there's always one sock missing when you do the laundry?" These kinds of mundane observations about everyday life are the foundation of his comedy, and they are all Reference. The Reference is how he starts a bit, but he quickly escalates it using Hyperbole, Wordplay, Character, and other Funny Filters.

FUNNY-WRITING TIP #14: DON'T FALL IN LOVE

You may think you have the greatest idea in the world, but don't fall in love with it. You may have to change it or cut it based on the feedback you get from an internal or external Editor.

Humor writing is closely tied to ego. When you write something that you think is funny, it hurts when you put it out there and it doesn't work. On some level, it can feel like it wasn't just your joke that bombed, it was your inherent worth as a human being.

Amateur humor writers often have one idea that they're very proud of. This makes them immune to potentially constructive feedback, because with so much ego riding on their one idea, they can't help but take personally any critical notes they might get.

Professional humor writers come up with tons of ideas, and are prepared to discard any ideas that don't connect with their own internal Editor, or the opinions of people in their inner circle.

The same principle applies to brilliantly written lines in a story. If they have to be cut, cut them. Sir Arthur Quiller-Couch famously said (though it's often mistakenly attributed to Mark Twain), "Murder your darlings."

There are gradations of Reference. The least sophisticated kind of Reference is the grade-D Reference. This is the "in-joke," where the writer uses a particular Reference that he/she knows will be understood only by a limited audience that's familiar with the Reference. This is also called a "room joke." On *The Tonight Show*, in the Johnny Carson era, it was called a "band joke." Members of the show's house band would laugh at the joke because they understood the Reference, which was usually something that happened during rehearsal or some other time that the studio and/or home audience didn't experience. In-jokes are fun for those involved, but they're easy, and don't have any practical application in professional comedy writing. Nonetheless, they pop up in Writer's Rooms frequently, and the keen comedy writer must always be on the lookout for them.

Local jokes are another type of grade-D Reference. These are jokes that refer to a particular geographic area (or trait thereof) that the writer shares with the audience. Local jokes can be very funny, but must always be assessed for their accessibility to audiences beyond the limited locality.

A grade-C Reference is the "callback." This is a Reference to an earlier joke told in your writing or in your performance. If you tell a joke, then tell other jokes for a while, and then come back to that first joke again, it's called a "callback." You're simply calling back that joke. This is very easy to do, but it's also a huge hit with audiences. Most stand-up routines end with a callback, usually one with some escalation, and it's a guaranteed laugh—that's why they finish with it. Watch just about any stand-up set and you'll see this tactic in action.

Slightly more sophisticated is the grade-B Reference, which points out things that are at the forefront of everyone's mind: the latest story in the 24-hour news cycle, for example, or other current event or cultural touchstone. It could be a holiday, the weather, or anything momentarily in the public consciousness. These are the go-to subjects of most late-night monologues, of course. If the current event is inherently amusing, many audiences will laugh simply at the Reference—you scarcely need to tell a joke about it. This is a relatively easy Reference because it doesn't take a lot of thought to come up with a current event, holiday, or other common Reference.

Slightly more sophisticated but still grade B (we'll call this grade B+) is a Reference to more obscure cultural tidbits that we've all experienced—modes of speech or ways of being that have become more prevalent recently. Referencing new or emerging clichés of speech is a popular form of Reference. *SNL* sketches employ this type of Reference a lot, using new-yet-familiar slang terms in dialog. Simon Rich, a former *SNL* writer who's written several short comedy essays, many of which are collected in the excellent collection *Ant Farm*, is especially adept at this kind of Reference. He references modes and structures of speech, conversations, social dynamics, interpersonal politics, and other loosely defined experiences we've all had. He recreates these things so perfectly that we recognize them instantly (that's how we "get" the Reference), no matter what the context. He also uses several other Funny Filters (and always a killer Subtext) to augment the Reference and create some of the best prose humor being written today.

Grade-A Reference, the most sophisticated kind, is any universal observation about everyday life that's yet to be pointed out in exactly the same way—a new thought about the way things are, or something that's wrong with the human condition. If it points out a shared weakness or human foible, something that the writer wants to change, it taps the core of all great Subtext and is the essence of Satire.

Most of Jerry Seinfeld's and Patton Oswalt's observational humor fits into the grade-A category, as did George Carlin's.

You find Reference by observing life and writing down anything you notice that you think other people might understand or relate to. There are so many things that you can share with your audience that make good Reference humor. You just have to take notice.

Some one-liner examples of the Reference Funny Filter:

> *Ever notice that anyone going slower*
> *than you is an idiot, but anyone going*
> *faster is a maniac?*
>
> —GEORGE CARLIN

Tip Of Man's Tongue Refuses To Relin-
quish Richard Crenna's Name

                    —THE ONION

Men don't care what's on TV. They only
care what else is on TV.

                    —JERRY SEINFELD

REFERENCE SUMMARY:

WHAT IT IS: Referring to something that readers will recognize from their own lives.

HOW TO USE IT: Come up with unique observations—everything from day-to-day life to broad issues about society, culture or life, and do so in a way that you don't believe anyone has done before. It might be helpful to use Jerry Seinfeld's famous "Did you ever notice…?" or "What's the deal with…?" intros (in your mind only, not on the page—these are now stand-up clichés) to get into the right mindset to come up with References that will connect with readers.

FUNNY FILTER 7: MADCAP

Madcap is physical humor. The prose equivalent is crazy, made-up words, the descriptions of slapstick, pratfalls, and other funny physical action. Absurdist references and seemingly random non sequiturs also count as Madcap.

This is where you loosen up and get silly. Very silly. Take your readers to Loonyland, where slaphappy, cartoonish things happen, and characters become unabashedly clownish.

Madcap is "seemingly" random because while the audience may perceive Madcap jokes as crazy, random, silly things, you, the writer, know you're conveying powerful Subtext. This is the only way Madcap works in

Satire. Even In Formulaic Humor, Subtext is critical for Madcap to be entertaining in any sustained way. Without Subtext, you have silliness for silliness's sake. If it's just pie-in-the-face antics with nothing intelligent going on beneath the surface, most in your audience will get bored quickly.

Kids (and kids at heart) are one of the few audiences who enjoy Madcap without letup, and will even tolerate it without Subtext. The prose category of Kid Stuff consists largely of Madcap: pratfalls, funny faces, talking animals wearing funny hats. Pure Wackytown. The green slime of Nickelodeon is a perfect example of Madcap humor without Subtext. Kids love it. The rest of us don't see the humor in it.

THE FUNNY FILTER CONTINUUM

You may have noticed that "funny words" appears as a feature of both Wordplay and Madcap.

These 11 Funny Filters tend to blur into each other at the periphery. Some are much more closely related than others. Parody (next), for example, is really just a unique subset of Reference.

This chapter is not meant to be the Periodic Table of Humor Elements. These are loose definitions to describe general concepts in humor. The end goal of these terms and tools is not an academic one, it's practical. They're here to communicate the concepts so you can use them intelligently to create humor, and also identify how and why your writing works or doesn't work, which is the central skill of a good inner Editor.

Madcap is like Shock; a little goes a long way. An otherwise calm, intelligent joke is often made a little more laugh-inducing with a pinch of Madcap. The insertion of an inherently funny-sounding word for a specific, inherently funny thing like "pants," "chimp," or "water balloon," or the clever insertion of a quick description of some over-the-top physical humor like someone falling over backwards or getting slapped in the face with a giant fish, can make all the difference in elevating a potentially drab joke into one that is more widely accessible, and actually has a chance to get a laugh.

Steve Martin wrote a book in the 1970s called *Cruel Shoes*, which used a lot of Madcap, as did his stand-up act. *The Onion* uses Madcap on occasion, in stories like "Secretary Of Agriculture Attends Diplomatic Meeting With Foreign Cabbage." It features a photo of the Secretary of Agriculture sitting next to a big head of cabbage in an official meeting room.

It may seem purely silly, but there's Subtext in a joke like that. Any high-level diplomatic meeting with the Secretary of Agriculture is something that most American news consumers probably couldn't care less about. So, he may as well be meeting with a head of cabbage. To state it more succinctly, Americans don't care what their government does.

Another way to interpret that story might be that our government is bloated. We have cabinet secretaries who do things and meet with people, but how is that making our lives better? It's absurd that humans got along just fine doing agriculture for thousands of years before there was a Secretary of Agriculture. In other words, a lot of what the government does is silly and pointless.

This is the beauty of Madcap. It's not only a Funny Filter that can help make any joke funny; it can serve to symbolize your Subtext, making a joke even funnier. Many times, the Subtext in a joke that uses primarily Madcap is "[Such and such] is absurd," or "[Such and such] is ridiculous," or "[Such and such] is crazy." The choice of Madcap as a Funny Filter communicates this kind of Subtext beautifully.

Since Madcap is concerned with physical humor, it's worth mentioning some examples from TV and movies, since they can shed light on how to best use Madcap in prose.

The Three Stooges and Jerry Lewis were known for their Madcap humor, but they rarely beefed up their purely physical slapstick antics with any meaningful Subtext. As a result, their barrage of funny faces and pratfalls was extremely unsophisticated. The Marx Brothers, on the other hand, used Madcap to great effect, most notably in their classic *Duck Soup*. By treating the serious matter of international relations to a full-on assault of crazy Madcap humor, they were, in effect, saying, "Isn't it crazy that humans think they can control other humans?," or "The world is a crazy place." Such simple, beautiful Subtext makes the onslaught of silliness so much funnier, in a profound and fulfilling way.

No one did Madcap better than Monty Python. Their "Ministry of Silly Walks" sketch is a Madcap classic that says, "Government bureaucracy is lunacy." Their "Election Night Special" sketch is a brilliant parody of election-night news coverage. It features returns coming in from various precincts, and the two parties getting most of the votes are the Sensible Party and the Silly Party. It starts silly, but when the mainstream Silly Party candidate gets a challenge from the fringe, the Very Silly Party, they really let loose the craziness. It's a masterpiece of Madcap and has aged extremely well. After almost half a century, this political sketch is still as relevant as today's headlines, especially when compared to American elections.

Seinfeld is one of the most sophisticated sitcoms that's ever been on TV. Most TV sitcoms rely on little more than Character, and occasionally Hyperbole, Reference, and Shock. *Seinfeld* used those plus Wordplay, Irony, and all the other Funny Filters as well. Where the show truly excelled was in its judicious use of Madcap. The complicated, tightly constructed plots and sophisticated Character, Hyperbole and Wordplay humor alone could have come across as dense and more intellectual than fun. But as soon as Kramer came bounding into a scene, pratfalling and making funny faces, the proper balance was struck, and the tone of the show was expertly tuned for maximum laughs. The show used Madcap as a garnish and always in service of the Subtext that came out of the various, interwoven plots.

Here are some one-liner examples of Madcap:

Racist Figurines March On Washington
—THE ONION

Here's something you don't often see
[makes a funny face and jumps up and
down].
—STEVE MARTIN

My biggest comedy influences are an
elderly woman and a recently mopped
staircase.

—Dan Guterman

The Subtext is clear in the first and third examples. *The Onion*'s is that mass marches on Washington are futile. Guterman uses grade-A Metahumor (Funny Filter 11) to comment on the very nature of humor. But what about Steve Martin? It seems at first glance like it's just a funny face and a physical stunt. But it's not. So much of what Steve Martin did on stage, from his persona to the majority of his jokes, mocked the idea of show business and entertainment. His entire act was meta, with such meaty Subtext that it did no less than help define the ironic tone that dominated the cultural landscape of the last quarter of the 20th century.

One watchword worth noting about Madcap: Beware of clichés. A lot of classic Madcap was so successful for so long that everyone used it, and many people still use it, and these are the worst of the worst clichés. I'm talking about things like banana peels, rubber chickens, Groucho glasses, and other standard comedy props. These things stopped being funny decades ago. They're painfully unfunny now. So, don't use them unless you're making fun of them.

MADCAP SUMMARY:
WHAT IT IS: Silly slapstick, inherently goofy items, non sequiturs, wacky words.
HOW TO USE IT: Make sure it serves (and even symbolizes) your Subtext. It works as the main thrust of a joke, but also as a garnish.

FUNNY FILTER 8: PARODY

Parody is making fun of another entertainment or information product. Any piece of writing, type of presentation, or anything intended to be presented to the public in any medium can be the target of Parody. That includes anything from a specific TV show, movie, book, magazine, or anything—all the way down to a church pamphlet, bus schedule or street sign. Beyond specific presentations or creators, overall media like movies, the stage or visual art can also be parodied.

Parody works best if readers are familiar with the work or medium being parodied. Not too many people may understand your brilliant parody of Inuit song duels. But if it's a more commonly experienced format or medium, or a popular (or at least reasonably well-known) specific entertainment product, you can parody it and be assured people will get it.

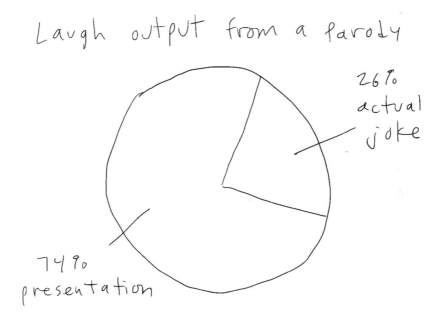

The Onion parodies a news website and the AP style used in most newswriting, and they do so in just about every article they publish. The *Diary of a Wimpy Kid* web comic and books parody, of course, a diary. Ian Frazier won the Thurber Prize for American Humor largely because of his brilliant piece, "Coyote v. Acme," which parodies both the Road Runner cartoons and a modern legal brief.

You parody something by mimicking its format, voice, or anything about it that calls it clearly to mind for your reader.

Parody is a powerful tool in humor. Readers will often laugh before they've even read any of your words—they'll merely see the context of your Parody (a design, presentation, or other framing device) that calls to mind the specific thing you're parodying, and that alone will amuse them greatly. You can see this phenomenon in action on *SNL* whenever they parody a popular movie. As soon as the lights come up on the set and the audience recognizes the movie's likeness, they laugh. They laugh even harder when a cast member appears, looking very much like a key character in the movie. Before a single word of dialog is spoken, the audience is already laughing. This is how effective Parody can be.

> FUNNY-WRITING TIP #15: BE SPECIFIC
> *A specific detail is usually funnier in a joke than a broad description, especially in the funny part of a joke, which (according to Funny-Writing Tip #8) should come last. Broad descriptions work well for Subtext, but in the actual wording of your joke, use specific detail for maximum laughs.*

With Parody, you accomplish two things. First, as with the other Funny Filters, you elucidate whatever Subtext you want. Second, you provide a kind of second Subtext, which is your opinion of whatever it is you're parodying. For maximum comic effect with Parody, the medium becomes the message.

In the examples above, Parody is used both to convey Subtext and lampoon the medium. Most stories in *The Onion* have their own Subtext, like, for example, a story about the government might have the time-honored Subtext, "our government is incompetent." But on top of that, *The Onion* is also, through its Parody format, saying, "modern journalism is worthless." This second layer of hidden meaning has very little to do with the core Subtext of the article. It casts a larger net, asking readers to question everything they read in the news.

In "Coyote v. Acme," Frazier casts a ridiculously logical light on *Looney*

Tunes. On top of that, he indicts our litigious society with his parody of the legal brief. His piece is brimming with Subtext: commenting on the ridiculous nature of cartoons, the pervasiveness of liability claims, as well as weak consumer protections.

There's one simple rule to using Parody. The writing or the design, format or framing device of the writing, must mirror the thing being parodied as closely as possible. This is what readers love about Parody; they like to see how close you can get it. If you're parodying another writer's style you must get it right, down to every syllable and punctuation mark. If you don't, if your Parody is half-baked, it won't be as funny.

Obviously, you don't want to mimic the *content*. That's the new element you're bringing to the table. You want to mimic only the form, format and/or presentation of your target. That might be the way it looks, the way it sounds, other quirks about it, or all the above.

Note how *The Onion* perfectly apes AP style in its newswriting. Note how Frazier gets every little phrase of his legal brief just right, so it sounds exactly like a real legal brief. Jeff Kinney uses the tone, syntax and even a hand-written font that makes his books look exactly like a kid's diary.

Readers love verisimilitude—when Parody comes eerily close to reality. The closer the resemblance, the better. (See Funny-Writing Tip #12, "Use Verisimilitude," page 72.)

I credit *National Lampoon* for significantly raising the bar on Parody. They put more thought into it, used professional designers and had a seemingly more serious approach than their predecessors, like *Mad*, to more precisely mimic the object of their parodies. Their *1964 High School Yearbook* is a great example.

A lot of humor writers think they can succeed with Parody by going half-way and getting the mimicry close enough. This may work, and will result in some people finding it amusing. But in order to generate big laughs with the widest possible audience, go all the way with Parody. Play it straight and don't wink at the reader. This elevates your work to a kind of hoax, where those not in the know may actually be fooled into thinking what you've created is the real thing, which happens all the time to

The Onion. There's scarcely anything funnier or more satisfying to the writer—and those select few in the audience who are in on the joke—than seeing other people fooled by a work of Parody.

How do you write Parody in a single line or joke? Think of other writing that's a similar size: a fortune cookie, a horoscope, a weather forecast, a newspaper headline or a tweet. There are so many. By borrowing a format like these and mimicking it so closely that everyone who reads it knows what you're referring to, you can harness the immense satirical power of the Parody Funny Filter.

Some Parody one-liner examples (from me):

> *The least scary man-turning-into-insect movie: THE HUMAN LADY BUG*

> *They should make an app that has car-trip games like License Plate ABCs, but instead of looking out the window you look at your phone.*

> *Book: THE COMPLETE IDIOT'S GUIDE TO BEING A COMPLETE IDIOT*

PARODY SUMMARY:
WHAT IT IS: Aping another entertainment or information product, format or specific presentation.
HOW TO USE IT: Use verisimilitude. Make your Parody look or sound as much like the real thing as possible.

FUNNY FILTER 9: ANALOGY

Analogy is the comparing of two different things and finding their similarities. The two things should be very different (opposites are especially good), and you must find many similarities. It's finding these connections between the two things and making the reader aware of them that makes Analogy funny.

Analogy, like Parody, is slightly more complex than the other Funny Filters. It provides another "hidden secret" in your writing. In addition to Subtext, the hidden secret in Analogy is the half of your Analogy that you keep veiled.

When you compare two things in an Analogy, you only want to reveal overtly one of the two things to the reader. The other is only alluded to, and readers are invited to add two and two to think of it on their own, thanks to your clues. This is a hidden nugget that's easier to discover than Subtext—it has to be discovered more quickly—but it's hidden all the same. If you mention it in your literal text, your joke could fall apart, much as it would if you stated your Subtext.

George Orwell's *Animal Farm* is a great work of Analogy. The two things being compared are animals on a farm and the major players in the Russian Revolution. The animals on the farm is the side of the Analogy that's explained and revealed overtly. The Russian Revolution is the secret side. At no point does Orwell break character by letting slip with any overt reference to the Russian Revolution, and he certainly doesn't say, "You realize this is really about the Russian Revolution, right?" If he had, the story would have lost a tremendous amount of credibility. He plays it straight, only showing the animals and their behavior. He never shows his hand.

One of the great achievements of *Animal Farm* is that readers in the know will enjoy the secret half of the Analogy, but readers who don't recognize the Russian Revolution will still enjoy an incredibly engaging book about political intrigue among funny talking animals on a farm. This greatly increases the work's accessibility. It's a far more popular book than it would have been had he written it without the Analogy Funny Filter. If he had simply analyzed the Russian Revolution and its key players overtly, the book would have been a bore.

But there's still more hidden meaning in *Animal Farm*: the Subtext. So, the two primary hidden messages in *Animal Farm*: (1) "these animals represent the Russian Revolution"—that's the secret half of the Analogy. And (2) "power corrupts"—that's the Subtext. This layering of hidden messages is one of the keys to engaging writing.

You can use Analogy in an entire work of fiction, like in *Animal Farm*, or you can use it in the space of a comedic article, like one of my favorites from *The Onion*: "Al Gore Places Infant Son In Rocket To Escape Dying Planet," which creates a wonderful comparison between Al Gore and his climate-change activism (the overt half of the Analogy) and Jor-El, Superman's father, and his warning to the elders of Krypton that their planet was in danger (the hidden half).

The Onion uses Analogy a lot. Congress is compared to a schoolyard, classroom or garage band. Romantic relationships are compared to workplace relationships. The list goes on and on. Analogy does not always have to be complex. It can be extremely simple and still be effective.

Whether it's executed in a complex, long-form work like a novel, or a simple one-line joke, Analogy must always be used the same way: the two things being compared must be very different; one of them must be revealed literally while the other must be kept secret; and you must make the reader aware of as many points of comparison as possible between the two. Each instance that calls to mind the hidden side of the Analogy creates a joke in your writing.

Examples of Analogy jokes:

> *Excited about Presidents' Day. Left milk*
> *and cookies for Lincoln.*
> —ALBERT BROOKS

> *Follow your dreams . . . you'll end up*
> *back home, but it'll feel like high school.*
> *Babe Ruth will be there, and you won't*
> *be wearing pants.*
> —ME

The overt part of Albert Brooks' Analogy is Presidents' Day. The secret part is Christmas. He packs in two—almost three—references to Christmas in this extremely short joke: (1) leaving milk and cookies for Santa; (2) an implied belief in Santa Claus; (3) his excitement, which we associate with Christmas, not Presidents' Day.

In my joke, dreams (as in aspirations) is the overt side of the Analogy. Dreams you have at night are the secret side. I make four connections, or clues, to the secret side: (1) being back home; (2) but it feels like high school; (3) Babe Ruth is there; (4) you're not wearing pants.

The currency in an Analogy joke is how many clues you can provide that link the two halves of the Analogy. This is where the laughs are.

Steve Martin's farting/smoking bit is a classic Analogy. It's one connection after the other, and you get the sense he could keep going with it:

> *"Mind if I smoke?" No, do you mind if I*
> *fart? It's one of my habits. Yeah, they've*
> *got a special section for me on airplanes*
> *now. I quit once for a year, you know, but*
> *I gained a lot of weight. It's hard to quit.*
> *After sex I really have the urge to light*
> *one up.*

The two things being analogized are Smoking and Farting. Farting is overt, Smoking is hidden.

Note how in a shorter joke, the hidden half of the Analogy is sometimes established overtly in the beginning but then never mentioned again. Once he establishes the subject of smoking at the top, Martin only alludes to tropes of smoking afterwards: special section on airplanes, lighting up after sex, trying to quit, etc. He doesn't say "smoking" again. He only uses these common associations with smoking but applies them to farting. This is a technique called "mapping," and it's how Analogy works.

ANALOGY SUMMARY:

WHAT IT IS: The comparing of two disparate things and finding as many comparisons as possible.

HOW TO USE IT: Keep one of the two parts of the Analogy "behind the curtain," while the other is laid bare. Every time you make a connection between the two by alluding the the secret half of the analogy in a way that the reader recognizes ("mapping"), that's a joke beat.

FUNNY FILTER 10: MISPLACED FOCUS

This is a Funny Filter in which the writer focuses on something other

than the Subtext, but something related to it, maybe a small thing just to the side of it, or a lesser-known aspect of it, to direct the reader's attention surreptitiously to the main idea by way of glaring omission.

Subtext, like always, is never openly stated. When you pretend to be unaware of your Subtext, it's like you have Myopia, and can't see the elephant in the room. Instead, you're intently focusing your attention on either the wrong thing or something that doesn't matter.

You can stir up a pretend sense of righteous indignation in the reader with Misplaced Focus. This works best with Subtext that's going to elicit a strong opinion from people, something very wrong with the world that readers not only know about, they care about it deeply, or are even angry about it.

By using Misplaced Focus, you can rattle the reader's cage about a serious issue and make them fume that something horrible is wrong with the world, expressed by your Subtext. They'll fume because you're not just ignoring the issue, not just failing to do anything about it—you don't even notice it!

When you pretend to lack awareness of an important issue, this is fun for the audience. It's you playing the dope, and it's widely accessible because it works for all ages, depending on the complexity of your Subtext.

Jonathan Swift's "A Modest Proposal" uses this technique to focus not on solving the problem of Ireland's poor children, but on the fake solution of eating them. While laughing at the absurdity with which Swift focuses his great argumentative powers on this wrong-headed solution, the reader is compelled to realize how tragic it is that there are so many Irish kids living in abject poverty. It compels the reader to ask, "Why is no one doing anything about it?" This, of course, is his Subtext. His seeming dismissal of the main issue (child poverty) in favor of his singular focus on this terrible solution to the problem (eating the children) inflames our righteous indignation.

Like Analogy and Parody, Misplaced Focus can provide a second hidden message in Satire beyond the Subtext: the Elephant in the Room. Often the Elephant in the Room *is* the Subtext, but sometimes it's not—it can also be a mere prop that's serving to elucidate your Subtext.

The Onion uses Misplaced Focus frequently. In the story, "Secondhand Smoke Linked to Secondhand Coolness," they bring to mind the dangers of secondhand smoke by focusing instead on how cool smoking makes you look.

When this story was published in the mid-1990s, authorities still argued about whether secondhand smoke was bad for people's health, and very few actual bans had been enacted into law (outside California). Cigarette companies certainly didn't think secondhand smoke was bad. People on both sides of the issue felt passionately about secondhand smoke. This story created laughter by inflaming those passions, focusing not on the real issue, but misplacing the focus onto something tangentially related, and far less important.

One more one-liner example of Misplaced Focus is this one, which came from Annie Goodson, one of my students at The Second City:

> *Mother Of Dead Teen Has No One To*
> *Update Her To The New iOS*

It's textbook Misplaced Focus, because it focuses on the Mother's need to update her phone instead of on the much more important matter of the death of her son.

MISPLACED FOCUS SUMMARY:
WHAT IT IS: A pretend lack of awareness of an obvious fact, brought to light by focusing on the wrong thing.
HOW TO USE IT: Think of something related to your Subtext but far less important. Then intently draw readers' attention to it, indirectly causing them to think of your Subtext. It's like saying, "Don't think of a pink elephant."

FUNNY FILTER 11:
METAHUMOR

Metahumor makes fun of other humor or the idea of humor, either by describing the effect of humor, using humor itself as a subject in a joke, or targeting a humor medium or specific attempt at humor.

Metahumor can have a tendency to appeal only to comedy nerds or insiders. So, an effort must be made to make it accessible to a wider audience if it's going to succeed.

If you've ever criticized a comedy performance, or wanted to mock a professional comedian or comedy writer or comedy production's attempt to be funny, or if you've ever wondered what humor is, and why people express it, you have the makings of Subtext for a Metahumor joke.

There are several levels of difficulty and sophistication in Metahumor:

The most sophisticated Metahumor (type A) mocks the concept of humor itself, finding absurdity in the fact that humans laugh at things. Type-A Metahumor is rare, and has a tendency to be a little esoteric for most readers, but if it can be made accessible, it can be revelatory. The Funny Filters most people encounter in popular entertainment are Character, Irony, Reference and Hyperbole, and a maybe a little Shock and Wordplay. So, an extra layer of surprise awaits the average reader, listener, or viewer who's unaccustomed to this kind of high-level humor.

FUNNY-WRITING TIP #16: THERE'S ONLY ONE RULE IN COMEDY

Once you try your hand at humor writing, you realize it's extremely difficult to do well. We can sometimes feel overwhelmed when we try to balance our instincts with the feedback we get from audiences and peers. Everybody has an opinion about what we're doing and how we could be doing it better. I realize books like this can contribute to that anxiety. Comedy writers hear a lot of dos and don'ts, which can stir up a lot of self-doubt. How do we stay focused on creating good comedy?

Just remember that there's only one rule: If they laugh, it's funny.

It doesn't help anyone to get overwhelmed. If you ever feel that way and have trouble coming up with funny ideas as a result, step away from the keyboard and forget about it for a while. Do something fun. When you come back to writing, remember that the goal there is the same. Readers just want to have fun. They want to laugh. If you can make them laugh—no matter how you're doing it—you're doing it right.

The next most sophisticated kind of Metahumor (type B) intellectually deconstructs comedy with no emotion or laughter. To plainly state the effect of humor without any razzle-dazzle can be very amusing to people. It evokes the Robot Archetype (or straight person). This is a character who reacts with far less emotion than situations warrant. (The Blues Brothers are a perfect example.) Deconstructing humor in this way—like I'm doing in this book, for example—can, at times, come off as funny, especially when the humor being analyzed is outrageously silly or shocking, like when I broke down the effect of farting and pooping jokes.

Slightly less sophisticated is type-C Metahumor, which openly derides well-respected comedy media, products, personalities, or clichés (or soon-to-be clichés) still in wide use, even by the comedically savvy. Targeting other people's perfectly respectable humor effort might be as simple as holding up a reputable comedic performance or piece of writing to some justifiable ridicule. When attempting this type of Metahumor, it's important that Funny-Writing Tip #10 ("Comfort the Afflicted, Afflict the Comfortable," page 64) be observed. You want to be careful not to mock an earnest beginner, or someone who might likely be crushed by such criticism. That's an undeserving target.

Writers embarking on type-C Metahumor need to be supremely confident in their own comedic ability before making a joke that involves tearing down someone else's legitimate attempt at humor. So, this takes some experience and some guts. It has to be done well or it will fall on its face.

The least sophisticated kind of Metahumor (type D) mocks comedy that's generally considered unsophisticated, or humor clichés that are no longer in vogue. These are the easy targets, like bad sitcoms, lowest-common-denominator Kid Stuff, mass-market comic strips and the like. Writers of type-D Metahumor might be getting easy laughs, but they're not making any kind of particularly daring statement.

(These different types, by the way, are just different ways this Funny Filter can be used. They're not a quality rating. The higher the "grade" letter, the more sophisticated the joke and the higher the level of difficulty in crafting it. But that doesn't mean perfectly funny jokes can't be written using any and all of these different types of Metahumor.)

Metahumor happens frequently in casual conversation. When we comment on a poor joke we've made, or someone else's poor joke, we do this to try to salvage a laugh from a failed attempt at humor. Late-night talk-show hosts do the same thing. If a monologue joke bombs, the comedian/host has a second chance to wring a laugh from the situation by becoming aware of the joke's failure, and commenting on it. Audiences love self-deprecating Metahumor (the shared fear of the entertainer's flop sweat is a strong motivator), so they're usually poised to be entertained by just about any reaction to a failed joke.

Steve Martin used a lot of Metahumor in his stand-up performances, mockingly referring to his act as "hilarious comedy jokes." In *Cruel Shoes* he used Metahumor in his piece, "Comedy Events You Can Do."

Metahumor in a simpler form can be added to other jokes or scenes. For example, not being able to tell a joke well is a funny trait to give a character. This was done with Marlin, Nemo's dad in *Finding Nemo*. This was also ironic because he's a Clown Fish, so you (and the other fish) might expect that he'd be great at telling a joke. There's an additional layer of both Irony and Metahumor in this trait because the character is voiced by Albert Brooks, a comic mastermind of the highest order.

A subset of Metahumor is Antihumor, in which the absence of humor becomes funny. If the context is right, and readers are expecting something funny, but the opposite—something clearly unfunny or the lack of anything funny—happens instead, this can also be very funny.

SENSE OF HUMOR

Every writer has comedy preferences and proclivities. You may prefer the humor from the Reference Funny Filter most of all and have an easy time writing jokes using Reference. You may find Metahumor difficult, because you just don't think that way, or don't find that kind of humor very inspiring.

Some Funny Filters will come more naturally to you, and others will be a struggle. Feel free to play to your strengths as much as you like. That's what gives you your unique voice and sense of humor. But I urge you to practice using all the Funny Filters, especially the ones you find most challenging.

When you condition your comedy-writing muscle to be able to write any kind of joke using any kind of Funny Filter, you increase your potential appeal. Your audience is no different from you. Each one of them has preferences for certain Funny Filters, too. So, when you use as many of the Funny Filters as possible in your writing, you'll blanket your potential audience, entertaining the greatest number of people.

Antihumor, however, is not for everyone. It can actually anger as many people as it entertains, so it's a tool best used with caution. When an audience expects humor but gets an overt lack of humor, they can sometimes feel betrayed. On the other hand, for those who appreciate Antihumor, it's an incredibly powerful tactic, and has the makings of cult appeal.

Andy Kaufman was well known for using Antihumor in his stand-up performances, like when he read *The Great Gatsby* on stage instead of telling jokes. I myself employed Antihumor in my daily comic strip, "Jim's Journal."

Here are some examples of Metahumor, in the form of short one-liners:

> *You like impressions? [Audience says, "Yes!"] . . . Why? . . . That was Socrates.*
>
> —Bo Burnham

> *I've been doing stand-up comedy forever, since women comics would get stage time right before they were burned as a witch.*
>
> —Jackie Kashian

> *My email was hacked but the guy was funnier so I left it alone.*
>
> —Albert Brooks

METAHUMOR SUMMARY:
WHAT IT IS: Stepping back and making humor itself the subject or target of the joke.
HOW TO USE IT: Metahumor works best with Subtexts having to do with humor, but can also be used as a garnish, or a small part of another joke.

CHAPTER 6 ACTION STEP:

Every Day for 10 days, write 10 funny one-liners, jokes, or funny titles for stories using each of the 11 Funny Filters. On the first day, try to write 10 Ironic jokes, on the second, 10 Character jokes, and so on. Put yourself in Clown mode so you can produce your ideas quickly and easily.

USING THE FUNNY FILTERS

I don't like to work alone. It's much easier to riff on ideas with a partner or a group or writers. The comedy bubbles up beautifully when heads come together, and the end result is usually far better than when I laboriously crank out material on my own. Besides, it's a lot of fun to sit around with other funny people and make each other laugh.

Before you can succeed in a group, however, it's a good idea to be a top performer in your own right. If you're not, you may be using a partner or group as a crutch. It's easy to rely on the energy of others to make up for your weaknesses as a comedy writer. And this isn't really fair to the others. When you become a solid joke creator in your own right, you become a more valuable contributor to a writing team. That's why I recommend focusing first on sharpening your own saw, so you can produce great work when you're sitting alone with your pad and pen. Then, and only then, jump into a comedy-writing team.

When you're at your personal best, you'll raise the bar for everyone else.

A group of individuals who are each operating at a heightened skill level is exponentially better at generating funny satirical writing than a group of mediocre writers using each other as a crutch.

There are a lot of other nuances and best practices for leveraging the power of a writers' room. I cover those in the third book in this series, *How To Write Funniest*. For now, let's focus on your own performance. It's best to hone your own skills before you start leaning on other members of a writers' room or group.

In this chapter, I'm going to illustrate three methods you can use to write funny lines on your own. Once you have writing partners or a group, there are other methods available. For now, there are three methods:

Method 1: Filtering. This is when you start with Subtext, then filter it through one or more Funny Filters to make a joke. This is the most mechanical, reverse-engineered method.

Method 2: Finessing. This is starting with a joke, or something resembling a joke, like a funny idea that came to you in a flash of inspiration, then refining and finessing it using your awareness of the importance of Subtext, and how the Funny Filters work.

Master humor-writing formula:

$$T_s \, / \, 1\text{-}11 \, (Ff) = J$$

Method 3: Divining. With no ideas and no notes, this is using the Funny Filters by themselves to drum up something funny out of nothing.

In all these methods, the core formula is the same. We are looking for Subtext reinterpreted through one or more Funny Filters. That's what creates a joke.

If you don't have much experience writing humor, these methods may seem clunky and mechanical at first. You may have thought writing humor would be fun, filled with inspiration and laughs.

The media often portrays comedy writing, and other kinds of creative work, as a fun and easy process, but that's not how it works. Writing comedy is a slog. I've never encountered a comedy writer who didn't recognize this unfortunate fact of the profession. If it were easy, we'd all be Tina Fey.

In time, with practice, these methods will feel less mechanical. If practiced enough, they'll start to feel like instinct, or at least a well-honed skill.

I'm going to go through the thought process of these three methods, exploring various ideas in order to demonstrate how a comedy writer thinks while crafting a joke. We're "live" here. I didn't prepare or vet any ideas for this chapter to make sure they were funny beforehand. I'm going to work off the cuff to give you a more honest portrayal of how this looks.

By demonstrating these processes this way, I hope to also show you Funny-Writing Tip #2 ("Quantity is the Key to Quality," page 22) in action. Not all of my ideas are going to be good. In fact, I may not have a single winner when this chapter is over. I might only get a couple of potential ideas out of it—if that—ones that I'll have to revisit later to see if I can punch them up. But that's all anyone can reasonably expect. No one spews comedy gold—there's a lot of junk that has to come out first. The trick is to keep spewing junk and then try to recognize the things that look less like junk and more like gold.

I've known and worked with a lot of comedy writers, and one thing I know is that while everyone's brain works differently, there are certain fundamental things we all have to do. Everyone has their own way they like to work, whether based on superstition or proven results, but all comedy writers, regardless of their work preferences, ultimately have to put words down, and these three methods are the most basic ways to approach this central task of writing humor. Experiment with them, combine them, or invent your own to find the method that works best for you.

METHOD 1: FILTERING

Turning your Subtext into an idea that's going to make people laugh will take some experimentation. Let's go through an example of how this might look.

If you've been carrying your notebook around for a few days, like I have, you probably have a few random thoughts written down. Or maybe you feel like sifting through some Morning Pages you remember being especially fruitful. Either way, in that pile of chaff let's say you find the observation, "Meeting an alien from another planet would be great and all that, but it probably wouldn't be very smart. In fact, it's probably just a dumb germ," which I just found in my notebook. Could this make for the Subtext of a joke? Let's see.

It has a clear subject-verb-object structure and expresses a simple opinion. So, yes, this can work as Subtext. It's not pointing out any human folly or universal injustice (except maybe the injustice of a dumb alien being a let-down after all the anticipation the human race has shown for meeting the first outer-space alien), but that's okay. For now, we only let amusement be our guide, and I find this thought somewhat amusing.

First, let's make sure we have our Clown hat on. We're trying to drum up some funny ideas here, so this is no place for the Editor.

We could try filtering the idea through the Character Funny Filter. The way the Character Funny Filter works is that we create a character with 1–3 simple traits, then have that character act on those traits, and this creates a joke. So, we can invent an alien character who's really stupid. Every time this character does something dumb, it will be funny. This tack happens to make use of the classic comedic Archetype, the Dummy.

If we try the Irony Funny Filter, we'll write the opposite of the Subtext, in this case, "aliens are super smart." This is nothing new. So, Irony probably won't work with this idea.

See how my Editor brain jumped in there? I don't want it to do that. As soon as I start judging my ideas negatively, I'm limiting my creativity. So, I'm going to continue exploring Irony.

Heightening contrast is essential in Irony, so simply writing about how an alien microbe is "very smart" isn't going to be enough. We want to heighten it as much as possible. Alien microbes should be educated, given the right to vote, or run for office. They're taking over Mensa. (Here we're also employing Hyperbole, continuing to exaggerate the alien's smarts to beyond the point of reason.) Perhaps there's a *Flowers for Algernon* story to be told about an alien germ who becomes a beloved super-genius. Now it's reminding me of *E.T.*

There's my Editor brain again. I want to compare my ideas to things that have come before, but not at this stage. At this stage I just want a free flow of creativity. I want to stay focused, pour out ideas, and worry about whether they're good later, and if they're too similar to something that's already been done, they can be axed later. For now it's grist for the mill, and will all get worked out when it comes time to assess these jokes down the road.

FUNNY-WRITING TIP #17: ONE IMPOSSIBLE THING AT A TIME

When you create a joke, you create a comedy universe in which something is either a little askew from reality, or you create a heightened reality in which one key idea is highlighted. In either case, with any joke, you can only have one "crazy" idea, or one impossible thing, per joke. If you try to give them two, your readers will end up confused. If we're going to laugh easily and freely, one comedic concept at a time is all we can handle.

We could try Parody and use a knowing reference to *E.T.* to make this idea funnier. A boy could meet and become friends with a super-smart microbe. And realize, too, that any time you're dealing with a talking animal or smart inanimate object (like a microbe), you're also using the Madcap Funny Filter.

When a lot of Funny Filters start piling up like that, that's a good sign. You'll want to continue in that vein to see if you can get some other Funny Filters working for you, too.

The essential guideline for Parody is that you want to mimic the form you're parodying as faithfully as possible, without winking at the reader. So, we're going to write about a very touching love story between a boy and his pet microbe from outer space.

> *In a real-life version of* E.T., *a local boy*
> *bonds with an empathic microbe from*
> *outer space, then dies.*

The smart-alien angle was feeling too far afield from my original Subtext, which I liked, so I went back to the alien being dumb and just acting in accordance with how a microbe would act (using the Character Funny Filter). I also added the Shock humor of the boy dying, which made sense given that's what would probably happen in this case.

Can we do anything to make this idea more relevant? How about any Reference humor? What do people know about aliens or, more specifically, alien microbes? They probably don't know much. I think they know what people would do if such an alien were discovered: they'd plaster its picture on the cover of *Time* magazine and it might be toasted as a celebrity. This could work because it might be funny to see that happen to something that's really dumb.

> *Alien Microbe Meets With President in*
> *Historic Intergalactic Summit*

This one came out in the form of a headline, which is fine. There's a good amount of Madcap there, which I always enjoy. But let's not forget Funny-Writing Tip #8: "Put the Funny Part Last" (page 58).

> *In Historic Intergalactic Summit,*
> *President Meets With Alien Microbe*

Let's try Misplaced Focus and see what happens. Instead of focusing on the alien, let's focus on the wrong thing, something smaller and less important than discovering alien life.

> *Now that science has discovered alien*
> *microbes, many Earth microbes are*
> *concerned about their job security.*

This also involved a little Wordplay and grade-B Reference with the double meaning of "aliens."

I'm feeling pretty lukewarm on this track. The main issue I'm running into is that I don't know if the wider public is aware that alien microbes might have been discovered a few years ago, and that's kind of important. The whole joke hinges on their awareness of this obscure and possibly moot science news.

That's not to say jokes have to be timely and relevant. I, for one, usually favor evergreen jokes that will be funny for years to come. But it's difficult to make one of those when your subject matter involves a specific news event.

I'll set these aside and look at them in a few days and see if I think they're any good. I can't possibly have any objectivity about them now, after having just written them.

FUNNY-WRITING TIP #18: KEEP IT SIMPLE

Don't try to overload a joke with too much exposition, informa-tion or too confusing a rubric for your audience to get through. Just use a Funny Filter to give a twist to your one subtextual message, and state it in the clearest, simplest way possible. Anything more and you're probably only going to confuse readers.

A couple of these attempts are under 140 characters, so I could tweet them if I wanted. A lot of comedy writers do that as soon as they write jokes, and I think that's great. As for me, I like to let them sit first. At this point, for all I know, the jokes might be awful—I don't trust my Clown brain, or even my Editor brain at this stage, because I'm too close to this joke. Worse yet, I might discover that my joke is identical to a joke some-one else already came up with, in which case I'll want to scrap mine. So, before I tweet anything I always Google it to see if there's been something similar.

Another example:

Let's say you had in your notes the observation, "It's funny how bus drivers wave at each other like comrades when they pass each other on the street while driving their busses."

This idea isn't inherently funny as is, but could be Subtext for a joke. If we create a bus-driver character who has one or two simple traits, it's on its way to becoming funny.

Let's say our bus driver is mean, hates everyone on the bus, and hates his life.

But we have to be careful—that's a cliché, the same bus-driver character we've seen in countless movies and TV shows.

There's that Editor brain again! But in this case, spotting a cliché might be helpful. It makes me realize that if we go with Irony, the cliché will be inverted, and therefore potentially a fresh take on this type of character.

(As you write more, you eventually want your brain to be able to switch between Clown and Editor fluidly. If you're just learning how to write humor, it's probably best to stay focused in Clown mode so you don't derail any progress by coming down too hard on your ideas.)

Let's go the other way with the bus driver and make him nice. This simple bus-driver character could be a one-liner on his own.

> *There was something seriously wrong*
> *with my bus driver today. He was nice.*

We lost our original Subtext there, but that's okay. It happens all the time—Subtext can get you started on an idea, but it doesn't mean you have to finish with the same Subtext. All that really matters is that you explore ideas and try to generate new ones that amuse you. When that happens, you might tap into a different Subtext, which can be just as worthy as the original. In this case, our new Subtext is, "I'm always suspicious when a bus driver is very nice." Now, if you look at this Subtext closely, you see it's reducible. It uses Irony. So, it's more of a joke. If you reduce it to its elemental meaning, the actual Subtext is "bus drivers are mean."

Is there an Analogy to be made here? Bus drivers are often sort of camped out in their driver's seats, since they're sitting there all day. What is that like? A homeless person camped out on a slab of cardboard on the street? Homeless people ask for change and so do bus drivers, so maybe there's something there.

> *Bus driver making smooth transition*
> *to homeless street dweller.*

> *I go by this guy every day who's camped*
> *out and asking for change. Then I pay my*
> *fare and take my seat.*

Yikes. That's awful.

There's a big attack from the Editor brain!

This is the kind of Editor-brain attack that can destroy the confidence of a beginning writer. "Yikes, that's awful!" can quickly turn to, "I'm no good!" and then, "I'll never be a comedy writer!" And that's not the kind of internal dialog you want to be having. Remember that all comedy writers write bad jokes, and forge on.

Maybe that joke is awful, but there might still be something to work with there. For now, though, let's take that helpful hint from the Editor brain for what it's worth, and move on to another Funny Filter. How about Shock? As soon as I thought of Shock, an idea popped into my mind:

> *When two porn-bus drivers pass each*
> *other on their routes, they customarily*
> *give each other a handjob.*

This might work, but it could involve two impossible things. The inherent Reference in the Subtext, which might not be very well known, and the zany idea of a porn-bus are the two impossible things. But it's making some small part of my brain giggle, so I'll put it on my Shortlist. It has Reference (inherent in the Subtext), Shock, Character, and Hyperbole (since I've exaggerated my Subtext to an impossible extreme—they can't give handjobs when driving by each other). So, it seems worthy at least of saving for later.

The final step of the Filtering method is to let ideas sit for a while and then come back later and assess them. At that point, you'll be using Method 2.

METHOD 2: FINESSING

Getting hit with inspiration and having a funny joke pop into your mind is a wonderful and lucky thing (which is why you must capture it in your notebook when it happens). But this happenstance can't be relied on as a dependable production method. A comedy writer works more like a miner than a magician.

The Finessing method works when you've got something pretty funny already, perhaps as a result of an unpredictable burst of inspiration, and you only need to refine it. If your notebook or Morning Pages contain a gem that's striking you as a workable joke, count yourself lucky, then use Method 2: Finessing to punch-up the joke to make sure it's as funny as it can be.

The other occasion when you'd use Method 2 is if you worked on some jokes using Method 1 a few days ago, and now you're pulling out the jokes you saved in order to give them a final polish. With this method, you need only assess your funny idea, and perhaps improve it by making sure it's clean, the contrast is heightened as much as it can be, and it doesn't have any logistics, spelling or grammatical errors. You also want to make sure you're clear what the Subtext is so you don't fundamentally alter what made this joke work for you in the first place. With this method, it's perilously easy to rework your joke into oblivion.

The first goal of this method is simply to make sure your joke makes sense, that it's given the best chance to succeed. Make sure you know what joke you're telling, and your reader knows what joke you're telling (Funny-Writing Tip #9, page 63). The second goal is to make sure it's structured to be as funny as it can be.

You're going to be in Editor brain this time.

I looked through my notebook and found a couple of these. Let's go through the process of Finessing those.

> *A killer adds a touch of class to his basement torture chamber with simulated wood grain.*

First, let's get square on what joke we're telling—this will better help us finesse it. What is this joke saying? In other words, what is the Subtext? Is it about a killer or his dungeon? No, it's a savage takedown of simulated wood grain, which looks awful and is the opposite of classy. The killer and his torture chamber are just tools to communicate this Subtext. I'm going as far away as I can from the idea of classy or pleasant or attractive home decor in order to say what I need to say about simulated wood grain.

It can be fun to deconstruct a joke after you've written it. You get a peek into your subconscious. (For example, how could I have known how much I hated simulated wood grain?) Through this process, you discover things about yourself you had no way to know before writing or deconstructing your joke.

So, what do we need to do next? First, I want to make sure the wood grain is clearly mocked. It might need more description, like "tiles," just to make sure the image is planted. I could cut some words if this is a headline.

> *Basement torture chamber classed up*
> *with simulated wood-grain tile.*

It's even tighter with "tile" over "tiles." That kind of attention to detail is important. We want jokes to be as tightly worded as possible.

If it's a one-liner, we could ascribe it to me or the killer character, but we might be better off concealing him more, and rearrange it so the funny part comes last, which is almost always a good idea:

> *Bachelor Tip: simulated wood-grain tile*
> *can class up your basement torture chamber.*

So now I've hidden some of the details a bit more, to let the reader better add two and two. Changing the voice from a headline to a direct call to action breaks it up and makes it a little more distinct from a lot of one-liners you hear.

This one-liner has Shock, with the moderate serial-killer reference. It has Parody, in that it's a spoof of a helpful household tip you might see on a website like askmen.com or its ilk. It has Irony, in that having classy decor is pretty much the opposite of having a torture chamber.

This one is sitting pretty well with me, and I'll definitely add it to the Shortlist.

Another example:

Let's say we look at a shortlist from a few days ago and find the joke "Dying Pen's Last Words Unintelligible."

This sounds like an *Onion* headline to me, and seems amusing enough. Let's figure out why.

It's using Analogy, comparing a dying pen to a dying person. Even at its very tight five words, it's making at least one connection point in that Analogy (dying people have last words, pens also make words). It's also using Character, personifying the pen and giving it one trait: it's dying. It's using Madcap, too, since a sentient pen is an inherently zany idea. Another Funny Filter I'm seeing is Reference. Actually, two instances of Reference: a dying pen, which we've all experienced, and a dying person, more specifically the cliché of a dying person in a movie or on a TV show when dramatic stakes hang on their last words. Finally, I'm seeing Irony. Unlike those movie and TV characters, a pen's last words usually end with far less drama. The pen's last words can't be seen, and the owner gets mildly frustrated and chucks the pen in the garbage.

So, there's a lot going on there. But what is the joke saying? Is there any Subtext? On its face, it doesn't seem like it. It's just a silly joke about a dying pen.

But when there's a Reference involved, there's usually some Subtext. The Reference here is the experience of having a pen die. What opinion is this joke expressing about that? Or is it simply referring to it? I think it's saying that even though the death of a pen is an anticlimactic event, it's still frustrating. The inability of the pen, and by extension the pen owner, to express their "dying words" is, on some personal level—at least to the pen owner—just as frustrating as it is on a TV show when the detective can't wrench a vital clue from a dying suspect. This comparison has heightened contrast because the two are at extreme ends of the drama spectrum.

That's what I'm getting from this joke. It's not earth-shaking Subtext, but it's enough!

The joke is already concise. My one concern is that the contrast isn't heightened quite as much as it could be. A pen dying and a character dying on a TV detective drama have contrast, but they're not polar opposites. Let's try to get there with a few different attempts.

Pen's fateful last words unintelligible.

The word "fateful" is turning up the contrast a bit. But it's still not a polar opposite.

Alas, I couldn't understand the fateful
last words of my dying pen.

We've put the funny part last now, which introduced some nice misdirection. But the biggest problem I'm having with this road we're on is that we're making the joke longer, which may not be the best thing for it.

What I might do with this joke is put it on another Shortlist and look at it again later, or maybe tweet a version of it and see what happens.

Ideally, before showing my work to an audience, I get feedback from some trusted peers. There's an involved process I use for vetting peers and ensuring that their advice is useful, but that, too, is a subject for another book.

METHOD 3: DIVINING

When you have no notes, or nothing in your notes that appeals to you, use the Divining method by starting with the Funny Filters and then forcing some jokes out. We're going to make a list of at least 10 one-liners (one for each Funny Filter) using this method.

We're in Clown mode again.

First, pick a Funny Filter. You can pick any one you want, but I'll just go through each one as listed in this book.

For Irony, think of things that are opposites:

- *Night and day*
- *Dark and light*
- *Big and small*
- *Old and young*

Now let's see if we can drum up any opinions about those things. I like night. It's exciting and filled with energy. By the same token, it's very relaxing to sleep then. There's more Irony. There might be a joke there:

> *I love the nighttime. I go out to clubs and*
> *get a good night's sleep there.*

On to the next Funny Filter, Character.

Think of some characters you know, or who are popular in the culture at large, and reduce them to 1–3 simple traits:

- *The Queen mother. Her single trait: She waves.*
- *Jared Leto. He has two traits: 1. He's a dedicated actor who alters his body in extreme ways for roles, and 2. He looks young.*
- *An astronaut. One or two traits: Astronauts always seem very flat and scientific when they speak—they're never excited or passionate.*
- *Your Dad. His traits: Let's say he does whatever your mom says.*

Now we need to make these characters act on their traits, which is how jokes are made with the Character Funny Filter. So, maybe Jared Leto can act on both traits at the same time:

> *Jared Leto is aging in reverse to prepare*
> *for a role as a zygote in his next film.*

Zygote is a funny word (Madcap), so Character, Madcap and Hyperbole are in evidence there.

Next is Shock. Shock is easy. We just have to be shocking. But let's try to be careful to observe the guidelines and keep the shocking aspects of our ideas mild, and let's also try to have some kind of Subtext.

What's shocking? Let's make a list.

- *Murder*
- *Racism*
- *People being burned alive*
- *Rape*
- *Genocide*
- *The guillotine*
- *Tearing out someone's heart and eating it raw*

Do we have any opinions about any of these things? They're all pretty horrible, for starters. The tearing out of the heart strikes me as the most workable one of the bunch. It's mild because it's not a real thing that happens every day (we hope), but that maybe savages did in ancient times. It's such a wildly inappropriate thing to do, it compels me to think of the opposite, to let Irony help out on this one:

> *A savage who tears out hearts and eats them raw is confirmed as the new U.S. Secretary of Defense.*

> *President Nominates Gen. Herbert T. Klinesdale Secretary of Tearing Out Hearts and Eating Them Raw*

That last one brings out some Subtext: that posts like Secretary of Defense, and the fact that we live in a world where war and conflict must awkwardly coexist with appropriate and civilized society, is strange and barbaric.

Next is Hyperbole. Hyperbole needs something to exaggerate, so we need to start with an opinion or some Subtext. What opinions do we have?

- *Dessert is delicious*
- *Slides are fun*
- *Bunnies are cute*
- *Depressed people are no fun to talk to*

Now, how can we exaggerate these opinions? We can take a dessert from that first one, and contrast it with something far larger:

World United by Delicious Cake

It's important to exaggerate the opinion beyond science or reality. Does this do it? Almost. We can inject some Character and Irony by exaggerating a slide from the second opinion on that list for another joke:

*10-year-old patron calls theme park's
new Stratospheric Super Sonic Slide with
600 double loops, half-mile sheer drop,
deadly G-forces and real lava "boring."*

Let's move on to the next Funny Filter, Wordplay. Wordplay is a great Funny Filter to start from scratch with because when you find an interesting way to play with words, sometimes interesting Subtext can come about in unexpected ways. Think of some common words, or maybe words that might seem like they'd be fun to play with, then start goofing around with them to see if you can come up with anything.

- *Bilbo Baggins*

- *The Reichstag*
- *Bumble bee*
- *Tumble-bum*
- *Tupperware*
- *Stink bomb*
- *Squirt gun*
- *Pellet gun*

Now, are there words that sound like these words that could be swapped with them, or ways to contort these words into new words? What about any similar words that might simply sound funny together?

> *Abominable Bumble Bee Haunts Local*
> *Bramble*

> *A homemaker is in stable condition after*
> *an unexpected Tupperwarelanche.*

There's a made-up word in that second one, but not much Subtext.

> *Toys"R"Us has banned the sale of semi-*
> *autoloading squirt guns.*

That's enough attempts at Wordplay for now.

Reference is next. Here, we just need to think of things that have happened in our lives, little moments that we think readers might be able to relate to.

Like, isn't it awful when you prepare a meal and then drop the plate when you're heading to the table with it? ("Don't you hate it when…" is another good way to get yourself in the mode of thinking up a Reference joke.)

Another idea: summer is better than winter because you don't have to put on and take off all those layers of coats, hat, boots, etc. One more: they say nobody gets enough vitamin D from the sun anymore, but they also warn against sun exposure.

That's a good amount of raw opinion to work with. Let's try to come up with a way to express some of these by teeing up the Reference Funny Filter, letting the reader add two and two to come up with the Subtext on their own.

> *Avoiding the sun yet getting enough*
> *Vitamin D are both important, so I drink*
> *8 glasses of sunblock per day.*

STRUCTURING ONE-LINERS AND JOKES

The way you arrange a bunch of words can determine whether they get a laugh or a yawn. It's wise to avoid clichéd structures like "shave and a haircut," or "da-da da, da-da da!," the ol' one-two punch, or any number of other standard joke-structure patterns that are equally difficult to describe in print.

The best jokes have an even tempo that sounds natural, without too much emphasis on any one part. If you overplay the part you think is funniest, you risk over-emphasizing it and coming off as desperate or old-fashioned (or Borscht Belt).

For example, Funny-Writing Tip #8 (page 58) advises, "Put the Funny Part Last." But in the Jared Leto joke I wrote earlier, I avoided putting the funny word dead least, because it would have reorganized the sentence structure too much and given the word Zygote too much emphasis: "Jared Leto is aging in reverse for a roll in his next film: a Zygote!" You almost don't need the exclamation point there because you can feel it. And the colon serves as a kind of silent drum roll. Both of these things smack of old-school night-club comedy, which is all a big cliché now. Avoiding clichés—including clichés of structure—is a rule that supersedes most others.

Next is Madcap. To get us started, some inherently funny things often used in Madcap are animals, funny hats, falling, goofy clown-horn sounds, pants, and chimps.

What do these things bring to mind? Let's see. I like funny hats (that's where I tend to go) and the pope has one of the funniest hats of all. He's such a great target because of the inherent Irony and Shock. (Irony because he holds a position that's taken extremely seriously yet he wears the silliest hat, and Shock because we're making fun of religion). With Madcap (large silly hats), we already have three Funny Filters and we haven't even told a joke yet!

So, how can we make this situation even sillier?

> *The Pope breaks out his matching conical*
> *gloves for winter.*

This one would be good with a picture showing the Pope wearing two-foot-tall, pointy (and impractical) gloves to match his hat. In that case, we could cut some words:

> *Pope breaks out matching winter gloves.*

After Madcap comes Parody. A good way to start with Parody it is to think of the last thing you read and try to parody that. The last thing I read was the order form from the photography company that took my son's school pictures.

To parody that, the first thing that comes to my mind is this form in the not-too-distant future, when child abductions are on the rise. Companies like this would send out order forms so you can select your child's milk-carton photo.

Okay. So, that's super dark, which adds Shock, but at least it has meaty Subtext.

> *It's that day of the year when the school*
> *takes all the kids' milk-carton photos.*

Let's move on to Analogy, which we divine by coming up with two disparate things that might have some similarities:

- *A terrorist attack and a common
  household errand*
- *A gathering storm and an impending
  visit from unwanted company*
- *A parent and a god*
- *Santa Claus and God*

Then we take one of those ideas and split the two pieces apart. Lay one out clearly, but only allude to the other:

*Suicide bomber had one other thing to do
but can't remember what it was*

To save humanity from sin, Santa sacrificed Chris Kringle, Jr.

For the next Funny Filter, Misplaced Focus, we want to think of something unimportant that we can focus intently on at the exclusion of something else that's far more important. What are some things that are really big and important?

- *Discovery of life on another planet*
- *The world ending*
- *An apocalypse*
- *A presidential election*
- *The world exploding*

Now, what are some very small things related to those big things? We're looking for little, unimportant details surrounding them, or maybe small consequences of them. For the world ending, there will be no more episodes of our favorite TV show. What will become of the fashion industry? For the apocalypse, there are the Biblical details, like horsemen, the Antichrist (actually, he's probably too important a figure in the End Times).

Let's work with that short list and see what happens:

> *Melissa Rivers offers fashion play-by-play at world's end.*

> *The Apocalypse will be a boon for out-of-work horsemen.*

That first one is more of an idea for a sketch than a one-liner. But that's okay. We're in Clown mode, so everything should be embraced.

The last Funny Filter on the list is Metahumor. Let's shoot for type-B Metahumor and deconstruct some comedy:

> *Hilarious comedy show elicits laughter, cheers*

And how about one more to try for a type-A Metahumor joke? For this, let's make it easy on ourselves and start out with some help from the Reference Funny Filter and list some idioms about humor or laughing that people have probably heard before:

> • *Laughter is the best medicine*
> • *It only hurts when I laugh*
> • *Laughter makes the world go around*
> [Actually, that's love, I think]

Okay, let's try working with one of those and see what happens:

> *It only hurts when I laugh, so I don't laugh, which hurts.*

Some word repetition in there adds a little Wordplay to that one.

So, that's 11 jokes written using the Divining method. They may not be great, but that's not the point. With the Divining method, we're solely in Clown-brain mode. That means it's always a good idea, if possible, to let the new jokes sit for a few days so you can forget about them, and then look them over later and assess them with a more objective eye (with your Editor brain), and perhaps use the Finessing method to sharpen them.

CHAPTER 7 ACTION STEPS

1. Write 10 one-liners, headlines or jokes using the Filtering method, going through any Subtext or other non-joke observations you find in your notebook or Morning Pages.

2. Go through your jokes from the chapter 6 action step and run them through the Finessing method to make sure they're as good as they can be.

3. Write 11 one-liners using the Divining method, cycling through each of the 11 Funny Filters.

PROCESS OVERVIEW

Let's review the step-by-step process for how to generate funny ideas, and how to repeat the process to consistently produce high-quality comedy.

All good humor writing starts with an opinion. A writer needs to have something to say. This opinion doesn't have to be funny, it just has to be something you have a feeling about. The humor writer generates this idea and then is compelled to express it to an audience. It can be an opinion about how it's no fun getting old, how chores are annoying, or something more sophisticated, like the idea that the human condition is a farce.

Usually, an opinion suitable for good Subtext comes in the form of a simple sentence: noun, verb, object. It must be an irreducible thought, which has no Subtext or hidden meaning of its own. It must be a flat, "on the nose" opinion.

This opinion, whether sophisticated, dark, uplifting or just small and silly, is the essential spark needed to create humor. The more astute and original your opinion, the better your humor writing is going to be. If your opinion is trite or contrived or, worst of all, a cliché, your humor writing is not going to be very good.

You can start with this opinion, or you can start with an attempt at a joke, and worry about finding and finessing an opinion from within the joke afterwards. Either way works.

There are two primary ways to generate the opinions you need. The first is to be struck by a lightning bolt of inspiration. This method is highly unreliable, so it's a good idea to keep a little notebook and pen with you at all times in order to capture those precious thoughts whenever they hit.

The other method is to sit in front of a computer or pad of paper and just start writing. Write continuously and without judgment for a half an hour every day. This is the Morning Pages exercise. As you do it, try to nudge your thoughts gently toward what amuses you. This is how you grease the wheels of your mind and churn up all sorts of humorous ideas and opinions that you didn't even know you had.

FUNNY-WRITING TIP #19: RUFFLE SOME FEATHERS

In Satire, if someone's not offended, you're probably not doing it right. The best humor has a little sense of danger, or mischievousness, as if the writer is getting away with saying something that shouldn't be said. Often this is at the expense of a humorless authority or other comfortable target. When a target gets angry at something you write, as long as they're a deserving target, consider that a badge of honor and a sign of success.

These two activities develop the Clown side of your brain. The Clown is the right side of the brain: the foolish, unrestrained, confident and prolific part of your brain where all your funny ideas come from. By carrying a notebook to write down inspired thoughts and by continuing to do the Morning Pages exercise, you prime the pump of your creativity until it's overflowing.

All good humor writers experience this sense of idea-overflow, and, as a result, feel compelled to get it out through writing. It's something they have to do, or they'll burst. Developing the Clown side of the brain is how you can generate this compulsion in yourself. It's relatively easy, but can take a few days or even weeks to see results from the Morning Pages.

The prolific and successful humor writer needs to develop not just the Clown side of the brain, but the Editor side as well. The Editor represents the left side of the brain: the logical, critical, organized and judgmental side. This side of the brain needs to be conditioned to sculpt humor by evaluating ideas based on the criteria laid out in this book. Does it have too many words? Is it a cliché? Is it comforting the comforted? These questions need to be answered, and any joke that doesn't meet the criteria for good humor needs to be either finessed or scrapped.

It will take some time for you to get confident using this process. The best way to master it is to practice it regularly. Here is a suggested schedule for that practice:

Every day, write in your notebook when an idea strikes you, and force yourself to do the Morning Pages exercise.

Once or twice a week, go through your notebook of ideas and your daily Morning Pages. If you see anything remotely interesting or potentially funny in either, take it out and put in on a Shortlist. For most writers, only a single-digit percentile of what they write will make it onto this Shortlist. That's fine. Some weeks you may have more, and some weeks you may have less. That's fine, too. Just remember that the more material you generate, no matter how good it is, the more you'll have to work with. And that's all that matters at this stage.

However, if you're consistently finding nothing interesting or amusing in all of your raw material, you're probably being overly critical of your work (relying too heavily on the Editor side of your brain), and it might be a good idea to get a second opinion, try to lower your standards, or go back to the drawing board and do more Clown cultivation. You might also try putting your work in front of readers, no matter how bad you think it is. No matter what happens, you'll probably learn something about your work that could help you improve.

There are generally two kinds of ideas that make it onto your Short-list: (1) Funny observations or opinions, and (2) unfunny observations or opinions. Each kind of idea is valuable. The former is clay you can shape into a joke. The latter is ore from which quality humor can be mined.

As you reshape and create jokes, your Subtext may change. That's okay. As long as your Subtext is saying something that you can stand behind, you're doing well. And if it's making you laugh, then you're in great shape.

Unfunny opinions can be extremely useful to the humor writer. They represent how you feel about a given subject, which is potential Subtext for humor. You can turn these ideas into funny writing by filtering them through one or more of the Funny Filters.

The Funny Filters process your ideas so readers can't taste your bitter, raw opinion. You want your reader to experience only the sweet, refined humor. Ideally, you want them to do this by discovering your Subtext sub-liminally. It's like feeding an aspirin to a child. You don't give the child a plain, dry, bitter pill to swallow. You crunch it up and put it in a spoonful of jelly. This is how Subtext works.

If readers wanted unrefined opinion, they would read the editorial page of the *Wall Street Journal*. They're reading your work because they want to read something funny. So, you need to hide your Subtext in a spoonful of humor. This is what the Funny Filters do for you.

Spend a few minutes every day trying to write humor. Do this by one of three methods: Filtering, Finessing and Divining.

In Filtering, you experiment with your Subtext by running it through each of the 11 Funny Filters. See if anything funny happens to it when it's looked at in the differently shaped funhouse mirror each Funny Filter provides. If something funny happens, add that idea to your Shortlist of potential jokes. If nothing particularly funny happens, you're either being too critical again, maybe your Subtext isn't elemental or astute enough, or maybe your chosen Funny Filter doesn't mesh with the Subtext. In any case. If it's not funny, just move on to the next joke.

The 11 Funny Filters represent the only 11 things that will work reliably to generate laughs in comedy. If you're working with good Subtext, one of the Funny Filters will work to turn your Subtext into a joke. If not, go through them again and make sure you're using each Funny Filter according to the guidelines.

If you don't have any Subtext but instead have a funny observation or funny line or joke that you've written, use the Finessing method. Now you're not looking so much at Subtext as you're trying to maximize the laugh potential of the joke. Go through all 19 of the Funny-Writing Tips in this book and assess your joke.

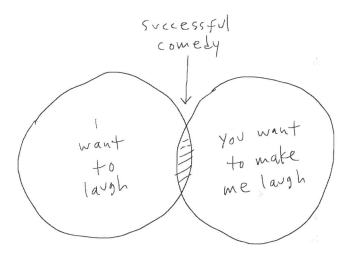

Does it conform to all the guidelines outlined in those tips? Is it a cliché? Could the contrast be heightened? Could you rearrange it so it has a better, less clichéd structure, or so that the funny part comes last?

What's the target? If the target is good (it must comfort the afflicted or afflict the comfortable), or if it's edgy because it gets tantalizingly close to the wrong target, move on to asking yourself what Funny Filters are being used. It's important that you know what joke you're telling, and how you're telling it. You need to be aware of what you're communicating and how you're making it funny for the reader. Only then can you have the kind of control you need to maximize the experience for your reader and get the biggest laugh possible.

Ask yourself, Could this joke make use of more Funny Filters? Could you layer them? Go through each Funny Filter and see if there's a way to incorporate some element of each without adversely affecting your joke, and certainly without adding too many new words. Most won't fit, but you might get lucky with a garnish. A slight pinch of Shock or Madcap almost always makes a joke better. And with some work, some sophisticated Wordplay could probably be applied. Could a character be involved? Could you change the format and turn it into Parody? Could you say the opposite of what you mean to find more Irony?

When you've beefed the joke up as much as you can, ask yourself, can any words be cut? Proof it to make sure it's spelled right and makes grammatical sense.

If you have no notes or jokes of any kind, use the Divining method, and go through each of the 11 Funny Filters and brainstorm jokes using each filter's inherent funniness.

After a few weeks of this, you've probably got yourself a few good jokes. Sift through the best jokes on your Shortlist and decide what to do with them. For what media is each idea is best suited? Do you have small ideas, suitable for no more than a tweet or one-liner? Do you have bigger ideas—ones that could sustain a short story? Maybe it's even worthy of a comic novel or screenplay?

Whatever the case, now it's time to get your work in front of readers, and find out what they think of it.

And whatever you do, don't fall in love with that one idea and stop generating new ones. Writers write, and successful writers continue to write, and continue to develop new ideas.

Work in other media, too. Don't just limit yourself to prose, stand-up, or any one medium. Writers who stretch their muscles in multiple media learn more and grow faster.

Continuing to write on a regular basis, adjusting your approach, getting reader feedback and then incorporating that newfound wisdom into your next piece of writing—in conjunction with all the tools we covered in this book—is the blueprint for becoming a great, funny writer.

CHAPTER 8 ACTION STEP:

Keep writing, and practice these techniques until you're Tina Fey.

What are the 13 most common mistakes in humor writing?

What are the 12 ways to structure a comedy story?

How can you dramatically improve your comedy writing by doing just *one thing*?

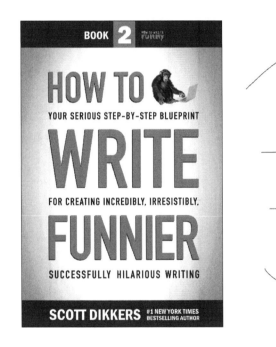

Find out this and more—plus learn to take your writing to the next level with short comedy articles, sketches, or bits—with *How to Write Funnier*, book 2 in the How to Write Funny Series.

GET YOUR COPY TODAY!

How do you get a job writing for *The Onion* or a late-night TV comedy show?

What's the secret to becoming a celebrated "comedy genius"?

How can you virtually *guarantee* your writing will be a hit with audiences?

Find out in Scott's

FREE EBOOK

Get yours now—along with free comedy tips, tricks and opportuities! Just visit

www.HowToWriteFunny.com

Printed in Poland
by Amazon Fulfillment
Poland Sp. z o.o., Wrocław

27209694R00083